new french table

new french table

Classic & Contemporary Home Cooking

Emily &
Giselle Roux

FIREFLY BOOKS

A Firefly Book

Published by Firefly Books Ltd. 2017

Design and layout copyright © 2017 Octopus Publishing Group
Text copyright © 2017 Emily & Giselle Roux
Photography copyright © 2017 Helen Cathcart

First printing

Publisher Cataloging-in-Publication Data (U.S.)

Library of Congress Cataloging-in-Publication Data is available

Library and Archives Canada Cataloguing in Publication

Roux, Emily, author
    New French table : classic and contemporary home cooking
/ Emily & Giselle Roux.
Includes index.
ISBN 978-1-77085-968-5 (hardcover)
    1. Cooking, French. 2. Cookbooks. I. Roux, Giselle, author II. Title.
TX719.R684 2017   641.5944   C2017-901785-3

Published in the United States by
Firefly Books (U.S.) Inc.
P.O. Box 1338, Ellicott Station
Buffalo, New York 14205

Published in Canada by
Firefly Books Ltd.
50 Staples Avenue, Unit 1
Richmond Hill, Ontario L4B 0A7

Printed in China

First published in Great Britain
by Mitchell Beazley, a division
of Octopus Publishing Group
Ltd, Carmelite House, 50
Victoria Embankment, London
EC4Y 0DZ

Emily & Giselle Roux assert the
moral right to be identified as
the authors of this work.

Commissioning Editor:
Eleanor Maxfield; **Senior
Editor:** Leanne Bryan; **Art
Director:** Juliette Norsworthy;
Photographer: Helen
Cathcart; **Food Stylist:** Rosie
Birkett; **Props Stylist:** Linda
Berlin; **Assistant Production
Manager:** Caroline Alberti

To Raymonde, grandmother and mother...

Contents

Introduction

How to Use This Book

This is the story of a mother and daughter's culinary lives and it reflects how their food has evolved over the years.

The journey starts with soups and salads. Emily was brought up on the colorful and wholesome soups that her mother would prepare all year round. The same ethos applies to Giselle's salads — never boring, always delicious. One of their favorite recipes is the tantalizing Fregola, Chorizo and Roasted Pepper Salad on page 54, which showcases the bold colors and flavors that they enjoy using and eating.

Next, we explore the southern French food that Giselle ate as a child and later cooked for her family and friends, then moving on to the imaginative, modern dishes that Emily now makes. Emily has introduced her mother to new dishes and techniques gleaned from her travels and her experiences in restaurant kitchens worldwide, but which all stem from her family's love of cooking and sharing food.

The all-important chapter on bread-making reflects their family traditions, with recipes that Giselle learned from her own mother, using her special Mother Dough starter (see page 228). The Rye Bread with Walnuts and Raisins on page 232 is a staple for Giselle, who makes it to eat at breakfast or to serve with cheese.

The book ends — like every good meal — with dessert. When it comes to the sweet course, mother and daughter agree that classic dishes are best, so this chapter includes many dishes that Giselle ate as a child and that the whole family still enjoy.

This is a unique record of a family kitchen and of cooking skills passed from generation to generation. And, now, with Emily passing on her professional knowledge to her mother, the story has come full circle.

Giselle

We are a foodie family — we love to cook and we love to eat. I grew up in a typical French household where we ate good, traditional, southern French food. I then married into the Roux family and became part of a cooking dynasty.

Food has always been, and still is, a big part of my life, but I had never thought of writing a book about it. One day when I was grumbling to my husband Michel that he had stolen yet another of my recipes for his book, his reply was: 'Well, write your own then!' I didn't take him seriously at first — I am a home cook, not a professional, so a cookbook seemed out of the question.

When our daughter Emily came back to live in London after attending catering college in Lyon and working in various prestigious restaurants we came up with a brilliant idea — a mother and daughter cookbook. We decided to combine my background of French home cooking with Emily's professional expertise and enthusiasm for the new techniques and contemporary tastes. I understand how the home cook feels and works, while Emily knows how to explain what to do.

We have both learned a lot and had so much fun coming up with the recipes for this book. We have worked through from the dishes I enjoyed as a child, to the food I cooked for Emily when she was growing up, then finally, to the meals we make together today.

Emily

Born into the most gastronomic of families and raised in London, my passion for food started at a young age. Playing with pots and pans instead of dolls seemed to be the norm for me. My mother always took great pleasure in providing me with fresh and healthy French food.

Many people think of French food as very rich, packed with butter and cream, but that is the northern style. The food of the South, where my mother comes from, is much closer to that of the Mediterranean, with an emphasis on fish, vegetables and olive oil.

I left the UK at the age of 18 to train at the renowned Institut Paul Bocuse in Lyon. After graduating I worked my way through the difficult echelons of a kitchen brigade in several Michelin-starred restaurants all over France. Some of these professional kitchens gave me the opportunity to travel all over the world. Today I love using the latest ingredients and innovative cooking techniques to bring a new twist on classic recipes.

In this book we show how cooking in our family has come full circle — my mother was taught by her own mother and she has now passed down her knowledge to me.

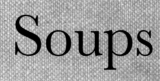

Soups

Giselle

Sometimes all you need is a bowl of soup: it warms you, it's healthy and what's more, it's a great way of using up vegetables, even those that are slightly past their best. I've always eaten a lot of soup and, growing up, my mother would serve it at the start of every meal during autumn and winter. She always had plenty of home-grown vegetables to hand and would make many different kinds of soup from them.

I've continued the tradition and Emily was brought up eating nourishing soups. I like to stick to one or two vegetables as a rule and let their taste shine through, rather than piling in a mishmash of lots of different sorts, then build up layers of flavor with ingredients such as ginger, chestnuts and walnuts. The flavors I use are more adventurous than my mother's and Emily has always appreciated them, even when she was a small child. These days, I'm even more daring and enjoy making things like Sweetcorn Soup with Popcorn and Crispy Chicken Skin (**see** page 32). But the same waste-not-want-not values that my mother instilled in me are still at the heart of my soup making and recipes like our Radish Top Soup (**see** page 28) are testament to that.

Green Booster Soup

This soup is packed full of flavor and bursting with vitamins; the perfect pick-me-up for a cold winter's evening.

Serves 4

1 tablespoon olive oil, plus extra for drizzling

½ onion, finely sliced

3 garlic cloves, crushed

2 zucchini, sliced

14 oz (400 g) leeks, sliced

7 oz (200 g) Tuscan kale

7 oz (200 g) spinach

2 cups (500 ml) water

1 bunch of cilantro, leaves chopped

1 bunch of parsley, leaves chopped

salt and freshly ground black pepper

crusty bread, to serve

Place the oil in a large pan or Dutch oven over a medium heat. Once hot, add the onions and garlic and cook, stirring continuously, until tender. Add the chopped zucchini and leeks to the pan and cook, stirring, for approximately 5 minutes. After they have released most of their water, add the Tuscan kale and spinach to the pan and stir to combine. Add the water, bring to a gentle simmer and leave to cook for 8 minutes.

Once all the ingredients are thoroughly cooked, season to taste and remove the pan from the heat. Transfer the soup to a blender along with both bunches of herbs (this may need to be done in batches), reserving a few leaves to garnish. Blend the soup until smooth, then transfer to serving bowls. Drizzle with good-quality olive oil and garnish with the reserved herbs. Serve very hot, accompanied by crusty bread.

White Winter Soup

This velvety white soup has a beautifully delicate flavor and makes the perfect winter warmer when served with roasted chestnuts.

Serves 4

2 tablespoons butter

1 onion, finely chopped

1 celery root (approx. 650 g), peeled and cut into bite-sized chunks

2¼ cups (570 ml) milk

1 cup (250 ml) water

1 sage leaf

1 thyme sprig

7 oz (200 g) peeled and cooked chestnuts

pinch of freshly grated or ground nutmeg

salt and freshly ground black pepper

Place 1 tablespoon of the butter in a large pan over a medium heat. Once melted, add the onion and cook, stirring continuously, for about 2 minutes until soft and translucent. Add the celery root to the pan and cook, stirring occasionally, for a few minutes, until it has just started to take on some color. Add the milk and water to the pan, along with the sage leaf and thyme sprig. Bring to a gentle simmer and leave to cook, uncovered, for 25 minutes, until the celery root is tender.

Meanwhile, melt the remaining butter in a small pan over a low heat. Once melted, add the chestnuts to the pan and stir to coat in the butter. Cook gently for 2–3 minutes, until the chestnuts are heated all the way through. Set aside and keep warm.

Once the celery root is tender, remove the herbs from the pan and discard. Transfer the soup to a blender (this may need to be done in batches) and blend until completely smooth. Season the soup to taste with salt, pepper and a pinch of nutmeg, then transfer to serving bowls. Serve the soup hot with the chestnuts on top.

Minestrone with Orzo

This comforting soup is a great way to use up any leftover vegetables that are lurking in the fridge. Feel free to adapt the recipe to use what's in season and what you have on hand.

Serves 4

2 tablespoons extra-virgin olive oil, plus extra for drizzling

1 red onion, finely chopped

1 garlic clove, crushed

1 carrot, peeled and diced into ½ in (1 cm) cubes

1 celery stalk, finely sliced

4 baby zucchini, diced into ½ in (1 cm) cubes

3½ oz (100 g) string beans, sliced into quarters

1 thyme sprig, leaves picked

2 cups (500 ml) vegetable stock

7 oz (200 g) chopped tomatoes

1¾ oz (50 g) orzo

1½ oz (40 g) baby watercress

1 handful of fresh parsley leaves, roughly chopped

salt and freshly ground black pepper

Heat the olive oil in a large pan over a medium heat. Once hot, add the onion, garlic, carrot, celery, baby zucchini, string beans and thyme to the pan and sauté, stirring continuously, for 5 minutes. Pour the vegetable stock and tomatoes into the pan and stir to combine. Bring to a boil, then reduce the heat to a simmer and season to taste. Add the orzo to the pan and stir to combine. Leave to cook for around 10 minutes, until the orzo is cooked but still retains a little bite.

Divide the soup between 4 serving bowls and top with the watercress, a scattering of fresh parsley and a drizzle of extra-virgin olive oil. Serve hot.

Mushroom Velouté with Roasted Spiced Walnuts

The spiced walnuts in this healthy recipe add a delicious crunch and a hit of spice. The walnuts can be made ahead of time and are a delicious snack on their own.

Serves 2

For the velouté:

2 tablespoons olive oil

1 lb 2 oz (500 g) cremini mushrooms, roughly chopped

1 large onion, finely sliced

1 garlic clove, crushed

1 tablespoon butter

1 cup (250 ml) whole milk

salt and freshly ground black pepper

For the roasted spiced walnuts:

1 tablespoon egg white

2¾ oz (75 g) shelled walnuts

pinch of chili powder

pinch of dried rosemary

pinch of ground cumin

Preheat the oven to 375°F (190°C), and line a baking sheet with parchment paper.

To prepare the roasted walnuts, place the egg whites in a bowl and lightly whisk to break them up. Add the walnuts to the bowl, followed by the spices, then mix everything together to ensure the nuts are well coated. Spread the walnuts out on the prepared baking sheet and bake for 5–8 minutes. Once cooked, set aside until ready to use.

Meanwhile, prepare the velouté. Heat the olive oil in a large frying pan over a high heat. Add the mushrooms and cook, stirring continuously, for 3 minutes, until lightly browned and most of their water has been released. Add the onions,

garlic and butter to the pan and reduce the heat to medium. Continue to cook, stirring, for a further 3 minutes, until the onions are soft and translucent. Season to taste, then add the milk to the pan and stir to combine. Just as the milk is starting to simmer, remove the pan from the heat and transfer the contents to a food processor. Blend the mixture until completely smooth.

Divide the velouté between 2 serving bowls and garnish with the roasted walnuts. Serve hot.

Split Pea Soup with Crispy Lardons and Croutons

This is a hearty and satisfying soup that is made even more tempting by the crunch of crispy croutons and salty bacon lardons. One bowl will keep you going all day.

Serves 4

For the soup:

2 tablespoons olive oil

3 leeks (approx. 10½ oz / 300 g), roughly chopped

2 onions, finely sliced

9 oz (250 g) dried split peas, soaked overnight in water, then drained and rinsed

2 teaspoons salt

6 cups (1.4 liters) water

5½ oz (150 g) smoked lardons

For the croutons:

3 slices stale white bread (approx. 6 oz / 180 g), cut into ⅝ inch (1.5 cm) cubes

1 thyme sprig, leaves picked

1 garlic clove, crushed

2 tablespoons olive oil

salt and freshly ground black pepper

Preheat the oven to 400°F (180°C), and line a large baking sheet with parchment paper.

To make the soup, heat the olive oil in a large pan over a medium heat. Add the leeks and onions and cook, stirring continuously, for 10 minutes, until soft and translucent. Add the split peas, salt and water to the pan and bring to a boil. Once boiling, reduce the heat to a simmer and leave to cook, covered, for 45–50 minutes, stirring occasionally.

Meanwhile, prepare the croutons. Place the cubes of bread, thyme and garlic in a bowl and season with salt and pepper. Drizzle over the olive oil, then toss everything together with your hands to ensure that the croutons are well coated. Spread the croutons out in a single layer on the prepared baking sheet and transfer to the oven for 15 minutes, turning halfway through cooking, until crispy and golden. Set aside until ready to use.

Place a nonstick frying pan over a medium heat and, once hot, add the lardons and cook, stirring continuously, for 4–5 minutes, until crispy and golden brown. Set aside until ready to use.

Once the soup has cooked, transfer to a blender (this may need to be done in batches) and blend to a consistency that you are happy with — we prefer ours to retain a little chunkiness rather than being completely smooth.

Divide the soup between 4 serving bowls and garnish with the crispy croutons and lardons. Serve piping hot.

Radish Top Soup

Never throw your radish tops away; they are packed with flavor and can easily be turned into a delightful and very economical soup.

Serves 2

10½ oz (300 g) radish tops

2 tablespoons olive oil

2 onions, finely sliced

1 large potato (approx. 7 oz / 200 g),
   peeled and finely sliced

1 teaspoon dried or fresh thyme

1 teaspoon salt

4 cups (1 liter) chicken stock

freshly ground black pepper

To prepare the radish tops, soak them for 15 minutes in a large quantity of water, drain and soak again until no grit or dirt remains. Transfer the radish tops to a salad spinner to remove any excess water.

Heat the olive oil in a large pan over a medium heat. Once hot, add the onions and potato, followed by the thyme, salt and a grinding of pepper. Cook the vegetables, stirring continuously, for around 5 minutes, until the onions are soft and translucent. Add the chicken stock to the pan, bring to a gentle simmer and leave to cook for 5 minutes, until the potato slices are tender.

Once the potatoes are cooked through, add the radish tops to the pan and cook for 3 minutes more, stirring occasionally. Transfer the soup to a blender (this may need to be done in batches) and blend until completely smooth. Check the seasoning and adjust if necessary, then transfer to serving bowls and serve hot.

Butternut Squash, Garlic and Cilantro Soup

The tangy combination of fresh ginger, garlic and cilantro brings this simple and delicious recipe together.

Serves 2

1 butternut squash (approx. 1 lb 5 oz / 600 g), peeled and cut into bite-sized chunks

3 garlic cloves, halved

1 tablespoon grated fresh ginger

1 thyme sprig

4 cups (1 liter) water or chicken stock

2 teaspoons sea salt flakes

1 pinch of chili powder

olive oil, for drizzling

1 handful of cilantro leaves, chopped, to garnish

Place the squash, garlic, ginger and thyme sprig in a large pan and pour over the water or chicken stock. Place the pan over medium heat and bring to a boil. Add the salt and chili powder, then reduce the heat to low and leave to cook, covered, for around 15 minutes, or until the squash is tender.

Remove the thyme sprig from the pan and discard. Transfer the soup to a blender (this may need to be done in batches) and blend until completely smooth. Check the seasoning and adjust if necessary, then transfer to serving bowls. Serve the soup hot with a drizzle of olive oil and a scattering of cilantro leaves to garnish.

Sweetcorn Soup with Popcorn and Crispy Chicken Skin

This combination may sound unusual, but give it a try and it's sure to become a firm favorite. The slight sweetness of the corn and the crunch of the chicken skin is a match made in heaven. Piment d'Espelette is a variety of pepper cultivated in the French Basque region of Espelette in the foothills of the Pyrenees. The spice has received AOC status (appellation d'origine contrôlée) for its distinctive mildly spicy, smoky-sweet flavor.

Serves 2

skin of 1 medium chicken (approx. 5½ oz / 150 g)

2 tablespoons olive oil

1 onion, roughly chopped

1 garlic clove, crushed

10 oz (280 g) canned corn

2 cups (500 ml) chicken stock

2 tablespoons vegetable oil

1 handful of popcorn kernels

2 pinches of **piment d'Espelette** or chili powder

1 teaspoon salt

2 tablespoons melted butter

¼ cup (50 ml) whipping cream

salt and freshly ground black pepper

Preheat the oven to 375°F (190°C), and line a baking sheet with parchment paper.

Lay the chicken skin flat on a chopping board and trim off any excess fat. Cut the skin into shards and lay flat on your prepared baking sheet. Season the skin with salt and pepper, then cover with another sheet of parchment paper. Lay a heavy baking sheet over the second sheet of parchment paper (this prevents the skin from curling up during cooking) and transfer to the oven to bake for 1 hour, until browned and crispy. Once cooked, set aside to cool.

Meanwhile, heat the olive oil in a large pan over a medium heat. Once hot, add the onion and garlic and cook, stirring continuously, for around 3 minutes, until soft and translucent. Add the sweetcorn and continue to cook, stirring, for around 3 minutes, until the liquid from the corn has evaporated. Pour in the chicken stock, bring to a boil and then reduce the heat to a gentle simmer. Cook for 15 minutes, stirring occasionally.

While the soup is cooking, prepare the popcorn kernels. Heat the vegetable oil in a large, lidded pan over a medium heat. Once hot, add half of the popcorn kernels to the pan and replace the lid. Cook, shaking the pan continuously, for 30 seconds. Once the kernels have popped, remove the lid and transfer the cooked corn to a bowl to cool. Repeat the process with the remaining corn, taking the pan off the heat after 30 seconds and leaving until all of the kernels have popped. Transfer the second batch of popcorn to the bowl, add the *piment d'Espelette* or chilli powder, salt and melted butter, and toss everything to combine. Set aside.

Once the soup has cooked, stir in the cream and season to taste. Transfer the soup to a blender (this may need to be done in batches) and blend until completely smooth. Divide the soup between 2 serving bowls and serve topped with the popcorn and shards of crispy chicken skin.

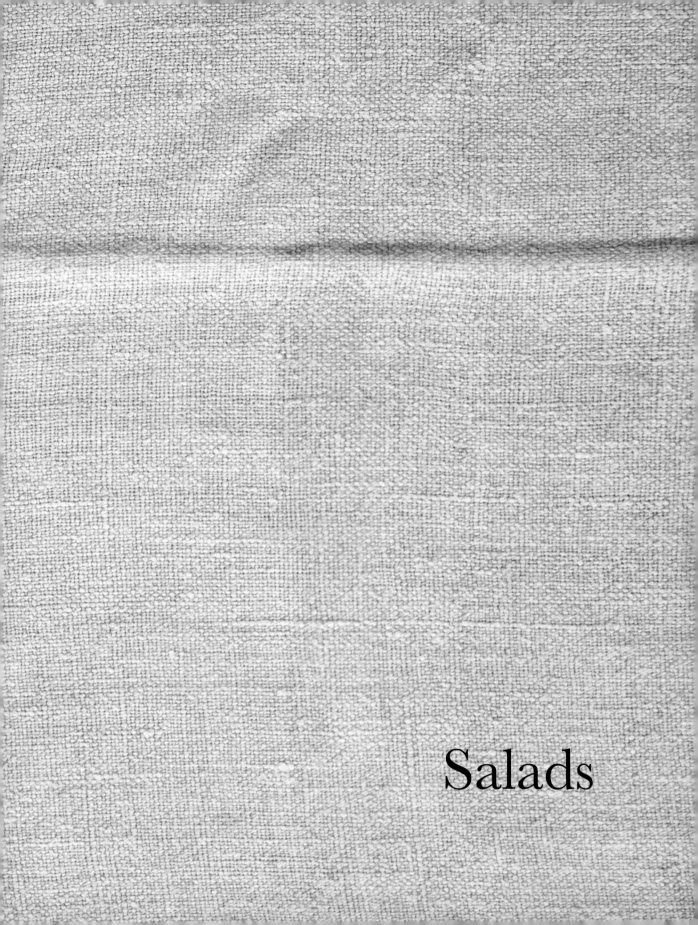

Salads

Giselle

When I was a child we ate salad every day in the summer to start a meal as we grew lots of different types of salad leaves in the garden. We used wild leaves too, and my mother would send us out to gather wild herbs and dandelion leaves — probably a good way of keeping us out of mischief!

I still make the lentil salads and Niçoise salad that my mother loved, but over the years I've tweaked and modernized them. I have always been a bit of a health freak and I like to use ingredients, such as quinoa that weren't around when I was growing up. I usually include some protein too, such as nuts or meat or fish, so the salads are filling — for example, my Carrot, Endive and Chicken Salad with an Asian Twist (see page 50), and my Fregola, Chorizo and Roasted Pepper Salad (see page 54). We eat our salads as a main meal now, which suits us all.

Fennel, Stilton, and Pine Nut Salad

This light salad is a refreshingly crisp and crunchy addition to any meal. Packed with delicate flavors, the blue cheese perfectly complements the slight hint of aniseed in the fennel.

Serves 4

½ bunch of flat-leaf parsley (approx. ½ oz / 15 g)

¼ bunch of cilantro

2 large bulbs of fennel

½ bunch of chives

1 oz (30 g) pine nuts

1 teaspoon aged balsamic vinegar

1 tablespoon lemon juice

2 tablespoons olive oil

2½ oz (70 g) Stilton

salt and freshly ground black pepper

Pluck the best-looking leaves off the parsley and cilantro bunches and place them in a large bowl of ice-cold water. Use the remaining leaves in other recipes in the book. Top and tail the fennel, retaining the fronds for garnishing, and slice it finely lengthways; using a mandolin will make your life a lot easier (but be careful of your fingers). Place all the fennel shavings in the iced water to crisp up. After a couple of minutes dry everything in a salad spinner, then place on a large plate or in a bowl. Slice the chives into small ½ inch (1 cm) pieces.

Throw the pine nuts in a dry frying pan and cook over a medium-low heat, stirring frequently until golden brown. After around 3–4 minutes remove the nuts from the heat and leave to cool on paper towels.

Whisk the vinegar, lemon juice and olive oil with a pinch of salt and pepper in a small bowl to make a dressing, then pour over the fennel salad and mix well. Delicately crumble the Stilton on top and sprinkle with the pine nuts, chives and reserved fennel fronds.

Roasted Beet Salad,
with Confit Shallots and Goat Cheese Shavings

Roasting the beets transforms this earthy vegetable into something silky and tender, bringing out the beet's sweeter side. This salad is perfect for a healthy and delicious lunch.

Serves 2

1 lb (450 g) red beets

1 cup (250 ml) olive oil, plus 2
    tablespoons for the dressing and
    extra for drizzling

1 pinch of dried oregano

2 small shallots (approx.
    2½ oz / 70 g), peeled

1 oz (30 g) walnuts, lightly roasted

¼ bunch of chives, roughly chopped

1 tablespoon good-quality balsamic
    vinegar

1 small hard goat cheese
    (1¼ oz / 35 g)

salt and freshly ground black pepper

Preheat the oven to 375°F (190°C). Scrub the beets thoroughly and cut off the leaves, if there are any (keep them to add to your salad). Wrap the beets loosely in foil with a drizzle of olive oil, a pinch of oregano and salt and pepper. If the beets are small enough and roughly the same size you can put several in the same foil parcel. Place on a baking tray and roast in the oven for 1½ hours (add 30 minutes for larger veggies), or until the tip of a knife easily slides through the middle of the beets.

Cook the shallots at the same time as the beets. Place them in a small ovenproof dish with enough oil to submerge them, then cover with foil and bake in the oven for 1 hour, or until they are a light golden color and very soft.

Remove the shallots and the beets from the oven. Leave the shallots to cool to room temperature. Leave the beets until cool enough to handle, then peel off the skins with the help of a small cloth.

Cut the beets into slices and flake or separate the shallots into a salad bowl. Add the roasted walnuts, roughly chopped chives and season with the 2 tablespoons olive oil, the balsamic vinegar, salt and pepper. Finally, grate the dried goat cheese over the top of this beautiful salad.

Niçoise Salad, with Fresh Tuna and Pesto Dressing

This typical Mediterranean salad can be disappointing with the dry canned tuna that it is usually made with, but this recipe is a tastier interpretation of a Niçoise, with fresh tuna and a pesto dressing.

Serves 2

5 oz (140 g) new potatoes

3½ oz (100 g) green beans, trimmed

2 eggs

a drizzle of olive oil

6 oz (180 g) fresh tuna

1 tablespoon black olives, pitted

½ green onion, finely sliced

6 cherry tomatoes, halved

2 baby gem lettuce (baby romaine), leaves only

1 handful of mesclun salad or baby mixed salad leaves

1 handful of small basil leaves

For the dressing:

1 teaspoon Dijon mustard

1 teaspoon basil pesto

2 tablespoons olive oil

1 tablespoon lemon juice

salt and freshly ground black pepper

Cook the new potatoes in boiling water for 10–15 minutes until tender, then drain and leave to cool. Cut in half or into quarters depending on the size and set aside.

Cook the beans in another pan of boiling salted water for 4–5 minutes until tender with a slight crunch. Drain and refresh in a bowl of iced water and set aside.

Fill a small saucepan with water, place the eggs in the pan and bring to a boil. Once boiling reduce the heat to a gentle simmer and set your timer for 10–12 minutes depending on how you enjoy eating your eggs. Once the eggs are cooked to your liking, remove them from the heat and refresh and peel under cold running water. Once cooled, quarter both eggs and set aside.

Heat the olive oil in a nonstick frying pan over a medium-high heat. Season the tuna with salt and pepper on both sides before putting in the pan. The fish only needs 1 minute on each side (depending on the thickness of the tuna) to stay raw and moist in the middle. Once cooked, remove from the heat and leave to cool. Slice the fish once it has cooled completely.

Delicately arrange your salad with all the prepared ingredients.

For the dressing, whisk the mustard and basil pesto together in a small bowl, then whisk in the olive oil, lemon juice and a pinch of salt and pepper. Pour the dressing over the salad.

Quinoa Salad, with Roasted Squash, Arugula and Ginger

Served cold or warm this mouth-watering salad will convert anyone to quinoa!

Serves 2

½ butternut squash, (we like the "coquina" variety) peeled, deseeded and cut into bite-sized chunks

3 tablespoons olive oil, plus extra for drizzling

1 sprig of thyme

½ inch (1 cm) piece of fresh root ginger, peeled

1½ cup (90 g) quinoa

½ shallot, finely chopped

2¼ oz (60 g) or a handful of arugula

juice of ½ lemon

1 teaspoon Dijon mustard

½ oz (15 g) pumpkin seeds

¼ oz (10 g) sunflower seeds

salt and freshly ground black pepper

Preheat the oven to 375°F (190°C).

Place the squash chunks on a baking tray with a drizzle of olive oil, salt, pepper and the thyme. Roast in the oven for 30 minutes, or until lightly colored. As soon as you remove the baking tray from the oven, grate the fresh ginger over the top and mix together. Leave to cool.

Place the quinoa in a saucepan with double its quantity in water and simmer for 15 minutes, or until the grains swell to 3–4 times their original size. With a couple of minutes of cooking time to spare, add the chopped shallot. This will tenderize the shallot and avoid the sharpness of a raw onion. Drain the remaining water (if any) and rinse under cold water, then place in a salad bowl with the arugula and squash.

To make the dressing, whisk the lemon juice and mustard together in a bowl. While whisking, gradually incorporate the olive oil until emulsified. Season to taste with salt and pepper, then mix the dressing through the quinoa and arugula.

Dress the salad elegantly as you like and don't forget to sprinkle the seeds on top.

Carrot, Endive and Chicken Salad, with an Asian Twist

This salad definitely "sticks to the ribs" as it is full of flavor and gives you a burst of energy for the rest of the day.

Serves 4

9 oz (250 g) boneless, skinless mini chicken breast

8 oz (230 g) carrots, grated

1 chicory, shredded, plus a few red chicory leaves to garnish

For the marinade:

½ garlic clove, grated

just under ¼ oz (8 g) freshly grated ginger

finely grated zest of ½ lemon

⅛ oz (5 g) chopped cilantro

1 tablespoon soy sauce

1 tablespoon sesame oil

For the dressing:

juice of ½ lemon

1 teaspoon Dijon mustard

2 tablespoons soy sauce

freshly ground black pepper

First, prepare the marinade as the chicken must absorb all those beautiful flavors for at least 2 hours. Slice the mini chicken breasts in half before putting them into a shallow dish. Add the grated garlic, ginger, lemon zest and cilantro. Finally, combine all the ingredients together with the soy sauce and sesame oil, then cover with plastic wrap and leave to marinate in the fridge.

After a couple of hours, pan-sear the chicken in a frying pan over a medium heat. You don't need to add any oil as there is enough in the marinade. Cook the fillets on each side for about 3 minutes, or until they are a lovely brown caramelized color. Remove and leave to cool to room temperature.

Meanwhile, make the salad dressing by whisking together the lemon juice, mustard, soy sauce and black pepper in a small bowl.

In a large salad bowl, mix the grated carrots and shredded chicory together. Pour the dressing all over the raw vegetables and mix together thoroughly. Finally, slice the mini chicken breasts into bite-sized pieces, about ¼ inch (5 mm) wide and spread elegantly on top of the salad. Garnish with a few red chicory leaves.

Grilled Baby Gem and Gizzard Salad, with Pickled Radishes

Giselle: This is one of my mother's favorites because it uses her exceptional radish pickles, although she's still not sure about the warm grilled salad! You can buy duck gizzards online or, if you can't find them, then use duck confit instead.

Serves 4

6 oz (170 g) sugar snap peas

4 baby gem lettuce (baby romaine), quartered

olive oil, for brushing

15 oz (425 g) drained canned duck gizzard

1 handful of tarragon, leaves only

1 handful of microherbs, to garnish (optional)

For the pickled radishes:

1 bunch of radishes, trimmed

1 pinch of mustard seeds

1 pinch of **piment d'Espelette** or chili powder

2 black peppercorns, crushed

½ + ⅓ cup (200 ml) water

½ + ⅓ cup (200 ml) white wine vinegar

2 teaspoons fine salt

3 tablespoons honey

For the dressing:

3 tablespoons cider vinegar

2 teaspoons Dijon mustard

1 tablespoon honey

¾ cup (170 ml) olive oil

1 tablespoon poppy seeds

salt and freshly ground black pepper

To make the pickled radishes you can either slice the radishes finely with a mandolin or a sharp knife or simply quarter them, which gives them an extra crunch. Place them in a 17 oz (500 ml) jar with the mustard seeds, *piment d'Espelette* and crushed peppercorns. Bring the measured water, vinegar, salt and honey to a boil in a saucepan. As soon as it has come to a rolling boil pour the mixture directly into the jar over the radishes. Leave to cool at room temperature before use.

Blanch the sugar snap peas in a pan of boiling salted water for 2–3 minutes until tender. Drain them and then refresh them immediately in a bowl of iced water.

Brush the quartered lettuce with a little olive oil. Place a griddle pan over a high heat and char the lettuce for less than a minute. Don't cook the lettuce.

To make the dressing, place the vinegar, mustard and honey in a small bowl. Season with a pinch of salt and pepper and whisk in the oil in a steady stream until it is combined. Finally, stir in the poppy seeds.

Arrange the sugar snap peas, lettuce and pickled radishes on plates. Slice the gizzards and scatter them over the top together with the tarragon leaves. Pour over the dressing, garnish with microherbs, if liked, and serve.

Fregola, Chorizo and Roasted Pepper Salad

Fregola (see photograph, pages 56–57) is a small Sardinian pasta that's rolled and toasted (resembling couscous). You can use it to make risottos, but it works perfectly in salads.

Serves 4

9¼ oz (265 g) fregola sarda

1 oz (30 g) sundried tomatoes, chopped

¼ bunch of chives, finely chopped

¼ bunch of parsley, finely chopped

1 green onion, finely sliced

2¼ oz (60 g) Spanish chorizo, sliced into julienne (thin strips the size of a matchstick)

1 handful of microherbs, to garnish (optional)

For the roasted peppers:

2 red bell peppers, cut in half lengthways, stalks removed and deseeded

a drizzle of olive oil

salt and freshly ground black pepper

For the salad dressing:

2 whole sundried tomatoes

2 tablespoons lemon juice

1 teaspoon grated lemon zest

2 teaspoons wholegrain mustard

4 tablespoons olive oil

Preheat the oven to 400°F (200°C), and line a baking tray with parchment paper.

To make the roasted peppers, place the peppers, cut-side down, on the prepared baking tray and season with salt, pepper and a drizzle of olive oil. Roast in the oven for 25 minutes until the skins are wrinkled and lightly charred. Remove from the oven, leave until cool enough to handle, then peel off the skin and slice into long strips. Set aside.

Bring a medium saucepan of salted water to a boil, add the fregola and boil for approximately 10–15 minutes until cooked through and tender. Strain and refresh under cold water. Leave to dry and cool, then place in a large salad bowl. Mix in the chopped sundried tomatoes, herbs and green onion.

For the dressing, whisk together all the ingredients in a small mixing bowl to create a light dressing. Pour the dressing over the fregola and mix everything together. At the last minute gently fold in the roast peppers and sliced chorizo, season to taste, and garnish with microherbs, if liked.

Lentil, Confit Tomato and Fresh Herb Salad
with a Mustard Dressing

Confit tomatoes are a great asset to any dish. You can prepare them well in advance (preferably during the season) and store them in sterilized jars in olive oil in a cool place for up to a year.

Serves 4

7 oz (200 g) green lentils

4 cups (1 liter) water

¼ oz (10 g) cilantro

¼ oz (10 g) parsley, roughly chopped

⅛ oz (5 g) mint leaves, chopped

½ oz (15 g) roasted hazelnuts

1 green onion, finely chopped

For the confit tomatoes:

12 plum tomatoes (approx.
  8½ oz / 240 g)

1 tablespoon olive oil

1 garlic clove, crushed

1 thyme sprig

1 pinch of superfine sugar

salt and freshly ground black pepper

For the mustard dressing:

1 teaspoon Dijon mustard

1 tablespoon olive oil

Preheat the oven to 275°F (135°C) and line a baking tray with parchment paper.

Rinse the lentils in cold water before placing them in a large saucepan with the measured water and a pinch of salt. Bring to a boil, cover the saucepan with a lid and reduce the heat to a gentle simmer for about 15–20 minutes. The lentils will double or triple in size once cooked.

For the confit tomatoes, quarter the tomatoes and remove the seeds with a small knife. (Do not discard the pulp and seeds as they will be used to make the salad dressing). Put the tomatoes in a small bowl and add the olive oil, garlic, thyme, sugar, salt and pepper. Make sure all the ingredients are properly mixed together, then spread them out on the prepared baking tray. Cook in the oven for 30–40 minutes, or until the tomatoes are slightly shriveled and reduced

in size. Remove from the oven. Be careful as the skins will become crispy and dry.

Pluck off the tastiest looking leaves from the herbs, then roughly chop the parsley and mint leaves that are a little too big for eating whole.

As my grandmother always says, it is extremely important to use each ingredient in its entirety. Wastage does not exist in her household. Place the reserved tomato pulp and seeds in a blender together with the mustard, olive oil and a pinch of salt and blend until combined. Alternatively, simply whisk the ingredients in a jam jar. This is a tasty, easy and beautifully textured salad dressing.

Once all the components are ready to use (cooled down), gently mix the lentils and fresh herbs with the salad dressing. Finally, sprinkle the roasted hazelnuts, green onion and the confit tomatoes on top.

Provincial Family Food

Emily

The recipes in this chapter are the sort of food that mum and I enjoy cooking together. As a family, we love southern French food — lots of vegetables, bread and pasta, some chicken and fish and not much red meat. People don't always realize food in the south of France is Mediterranean in style, using olive oil, instead of the rich butter and cream popular in the north of the country.

We still make the recipes I enjoyed as a child but now I might adapt and update them. For instance, *Lapin à la Moutarde* (see page 88) is a classic that mum ate as a child and used to cook for me in my childhood. Hers is a traditional, rustic recipe and very good. My take on it (see page 82) is slightly more refined, but still retains all of the elements that make the original so special. Other treasured dishes are Tomato Tart (see page 75), *Tian de Legumes* (see page 66), and of course *Escargots à la Bourguignonne* (see page 78).

Tian de Legumes

This beautiful dish of layered roasted vegetables is a real showstopper, especially when placed in the center of a table so that everyone can serve themselves. Equally delicious as a main course or to sit beside a roast of meat, this will have even the most committed carnivores coming back for more.

Serves 4–6

4 large tomatoes, cut into ¼ inch (5 mm) slices

2 red onions, cut into ¼ inch (5 mm) slices

1 green zucchini, cut into ¼ inch (5 mm) slices

1 yellow zucchini, cut into ¼ inch (5 mm) slices

2 eggplant, cut into ¼ inch (5 mm) slices

2 teaspoons sea salt

2 garlic cloves, roughly chopped

1 pinch of **piment d'Espelette** or chili powder

1 thyme sprig, leaves picked

5 tablespoons olive oil

½ cup (40 g) Parmesan, grated (optional)

salt and freshly ground black pepper

Preheat the oven to 400°F (200°C).

Place all of the sliced vegetables in a colander and scatter over the sea salt. Set aside for at least 20 minutes to render any excess water. Brush off the excess salt with paper towels and set aside.

Bring a large pan of water to a boil over a medium heat. Add the sliced vegetables and blanch for 40 seconds, then drain and lay on paper towels to dry. Once dry, place all of the vegetables in a large bowl with the garlic, *piment d'Espelette* or chili powder, thyme and olive oil. Season generously, then use your hands to toss the vegetables and ensure they are all well coated in the oil and spices.

Arrange the vegetables in tight vertical rows in a large baking dish, working from the outside of the dish into the center and alternating them to create an attractive pattern. Transfer to the oven to bake for 40 minutes, until cooked through and crispy on top. If using, scatter over the Parmesan halfway through the cooking time. Serve hot.

Socca

These chickpea flatbreads are simple to make and are an easy alternative to homemade leavened breads. They make a tasty snack served with Tapenade (see page 96), sundried tomato spread or pesto and are a great accompaniment to soups or stews.

Serves 4

9 oz (250 g) chickpea flour, or gram

1 cup (250 ml) water

5 tablespoons olive oil, plus extra for greasing

½ teaspoon chopped rosemary

salt and freshly ground black pepper

Sift the flour into a large bowl and make a well in the center. Gradually pour the water into the well, whisking the flour into the water continuously. Once the water is fully incorporated, add the olive oil and rosemary and season to taste. Whisk again to combine, then cover the bowl with plastic wrap and set aside to rest at room temperature for 1 hour.

Once the mixture has rested, give it a final whisk to ensure the flour is fully incorporated and that the mixture contains no lumps.

Lightly grease a large frying pan with oil and place it over a medium heat. Once the pan is hot, pour a ladleful of the batter into the pan, swirling to cover the entire base. Cook for 2 minutes, until bubbles start to appear in the batter, then carefully flip the flatbread over in the pan and cook for another minute on the reverse side. Keep warm in a low oven while you make the remaining flatbreads (the mixture makes 5 or 6, depending on size).

Slice the breads into wedges and serve hot with tapenade, sundried tomato spread or pesto, or to accompany soups or stews.

Whole Roast Pigeon, with Peaches, Turnips and Sage

This roast is bursting with bold flavor combinations and the subtle sweetness of ripe peaches combined with the delicate earthiness of turnip elevates it to another level.

Serves 2

2 tablespoons olive oil

2 whole wood pigeons

2 thyme sprigs

2 garlic cloves, crushed

3 tablespoons butter

2 juicy peaches or nectarines, peeled and cut into bite-sized pieces

2 baby gem lettuce (baby romaine), halved

1 cup (250 ml) chicken stock

4 medium-sized turnips, halved

4 sage leaves, finely chopped

salt and freshly ground black pepper

Preheat the oven to 350°F (180°C).

Heat a tablespoon of the olive oil in a large frying pan over a medium-high heat. Place the pigeons breast-side down into the pan, and turn every 3 minutes to evenly sear and achieve a golden color all over. Transfer the birds, breast-side up, to a roasting pan. Season the pigeons with salt and pepper and fill their cavities with a sprig of thyme, crushed garlic clove and 1 tablespoon of butter. Transfer to the oven and roast for 10–12 minutes, depending on the size of your birds. Once cooked, remove from the oven and set aside to rest for at least 5 minutes before carving.

Meanwhile, heat the remaining olive oil in a large frying pan and, once hot, add the peaches or nectarines and lettuce halves. Cook for 2–3 minutes, turning occasionally, until the fruit is lightly caramelized and the lettuce is lightly charred. Remove from the heat and set aside.

Place the stock and remaining tablespoon of butter in a medium saucepan over a high heat. Bring just to a boil, then reduce the heat to a simmer and add the turnips to the pan. Cook, covered, for 6–8 minutes, then remove the lid and cook for a further 4 minutes, until the liquid is reduced and the turnips are beautifully glazed.

Place each pigeon on a serving plate and arrange the peaches, lettuce and turnips around the plates. Spoon over the reduced sauce and scatter the sage leaves over the vegetables. Serve hot.

Le Crespeou

This is a layered omelette cake with beautiful colors and distinct flavors. Don't shy away from the work involved as it's well worth it. This is delicious eaten warm or cold.

Serves 6

For the green omelette:

2 tablespoons olive oil

1 garlic clove, finely chopped

10 oz (280 g) baby spinach

4 eggs, beaten

salt and freshly ground black pepper

For the yellow omelette:

1 yellow bell pepper, halved, deseeded and coarsely grated

2 tablespoons olive oil

1 pinch of curry powder

4 eggs, beaten

For the mushroom omelette:

2 tablespoons olive oil

7 oz (200 g) white mushrooms, finely sliced

1 teaspoon dried thyme

4 eggs, beaten

⅓ cup (30 g) fresh grated Parmesan

For the red omelette:

3 ripe tomatoes

2 tablespoons olive oil

1 red onion, diced into ½ inch (1 cm) cubes

1 pinch of cayenne pepper

4 eggs, beaten

Start by preparing the filling for each omelette.

For the **green omelette**, heat half the olive oil in a frying pan over a medium heat and, once hot, add the garlic. Cook, stirring continuously, for 1 minute, until just starting to color, then add the spinach and season with salt and pepper. Cook, stirring, for 3 minutes, until the spinach is completely wilted. Transfer the spinach to a bowl and set aside until cool enough to handle. Once cooled, squeeze the spinach in your hands to remove any excess water, then roughly chop. Set aside.

For the **yellow omelette**, lay the grated pepper in a piece of paper towels and squeeze tightly to remove any liquid. Heat half the olive oil in a frying pan over a medium heat and, once hot, add the pepper. Cook, stirring continuously, for 3 minutes, until tender, then add the curry powder and season to taste. Transfer to a plate lined with paper towels and set aside until ready to serve.

For the **mushroom omelette**, heat half the oil in a frying pan and, once hot, add the mushrooms and thyme. Cook, stirring continuously, for 4–5 minutes, until the mushrooms are soft and have rendered all of their water. Season to taste and set aside until ready to use.

Continues next page...

Le Crespeou **continued**

For the **red omelette**, lightly score crosses into the base of the tomatoes then place in a pan of boiling water for 20–30 seconds, until the tomato skins start to split. Drain the tomatoes, then transfer to a bowl of iced water until cool enough to handle. Peel the tomatoes and discard the skin, then slice into quarters and deseed with a spoon. Chop the tomato quarters into a ½ in (1 cm) dice and set aside.

Heat half the oil in a frying pan over a medium heat and, once hot, add the onion. Cook, stirring continuously, for 2 minutes, until just tender. Add the tomatoes and cayenne pepper to the pan and season to taste. Cook for 1 minute more, then transfer to a plate lined with paper towels and set aside until ready to use.

To cook the omelettes, place the beaten eggs in 4 separate bowls and add one set of your prepared fillings and some salt and pepper to each. Working with one omelette at a time, heat 1 tablespoon of oil in a frying pan and, once hot, pour in your omelette mix, swirling to ensure it coats the base of the pan. Cook for 3 minutes,

until the edges are firm, then use a spatula to carefully flip the omelette and cook for a further 2 minutes on the reverse. For the mushroom omelette, add the grated Parmesan to the pan just before the omelette is flipped. Once golden on both sides, transfer the omelettes to a plate stacking them one on top of the other.

Serve the *crespeou* warm or cold with a crisp green salad.

Tomato Tart

This summery tomato tart is deliciously fresh and makes a wonderfully light alternative to pizza. Perfect for sharing with family and friends over a glass of wine.

makes a 9½ × 7 inch (24 × 18 cm) tart

12 oz (350 g) cherry tomatoes, halved or quartered, depending on size

3 tablespoons olive oil, plus extra for greasing and drizzling

6 small shallots, peeled and cut into ¼ inch (5 mm) slices

9 oz (250 g) puff pastry

⅓ cup (100 g) crème fraîche

2 tablespoons wholegrain mustard

5 basil leaves

½ oz (15 g) pine nuts, toasted

⅓ cup (30 g) Parmesan shavings

salt and freshly ground black pepper

Preheat the oven to 350°F (180°C).

Place the tomatoes in a colander and generously sprinkle with salt. Set aside for 30 minutes to render any excess water. This will prevent your finished tart from being soggy.

Generously grease a baking sheet with olive oil and lay the sliced shallots over it in a single layer. Transfer to the oven and bake for 15 minutes, until just golden. Set aside until ready to use.

Lightly grease a 9½ × 7 in (24 × 18 cm) lipped baking tray with olive oil and line with parchment paper. On a lightly floured surface, roll out the puff pastry to the size of your tray, then transfer to the tray and lightly prick the base and sides. Cook in the oven for 10 minutes, until just golden. Remove from the oven and lower the temperature to 300°F (150°C).

In a small bowl, whisk the crème fraîche and mustard together until just combined. Leaving a 1 in (2.5 cm) gap all around the edge of the pastry, spread the crème fraîche and mustard mix over the base of the tart. Scatter the basil leaves over the crème fraîche, then top with the tomatoes and shallots, arranging them in an attractive pattern. Return the tart to the oven to bake for another 20 minutes, until the pastry is golden and well risen and the tomatoes are soft.

Leave the tart to cool slightly, then garnish with pine nuts, Parmesan shavings and a drizzle of olive oil before serving.

Stuffed Zucchini

Zucchini are often overlooked, but when treated well they are packed with flavor. Here they are stuffed with a mixture of lean minced pork and sausage meat and served with a deliciously rich veal gravy.

Serves 4

2 large zucchini

1 teaspoon olive oil

1 carrot, peeled and
    finely diced

1 onion, finely chopped

1 leek, finely chopped

1 garlic clove, crushed

5½ oz (150 g) sausage meat

5½ oz (150 g) minced pork loin

½ cup (50 g) Parmesan, grated

1 egg yolk

1¾ oz (50 g) mint leaves, roughly
    chopped

½ + ⅓ cup (200 ml) white wine

1¾ cup (400 ml) veal stock

salt and freshly ground black pepper

Preheat the oven to 350°F (180°C).

Trim the zucchini and slice off the top third of their length. Finely dice the removed portions of zucchini and set aside for later. Using a small spoon, scoop out the center of the remaining zucchini to create hollow tubes, but leaving the base intact. Place the scooped innards of the zucchini in a bowl with the diced zucchini and set aside to use later.

Heat the oil in a large pan over a medium heat. Once hot, add the carrot, onion, leek, garlic and reserved zucchini and stir-fry for 3 minutes, until tender. Set aside until cool enough to handle.

Bring a pan of salted water to a boil over a medium heat and add the zucchini tubes. Cook for 1 minute, then drain and immediately submerge in iced water to stop the cooking process. Set aside until ready to use.

Place the sausage meat and minced pork loin in a large bowl with the stir-fried vegetables, egg yolk and mint and season generously. Using your hands, mix all of the ingredients together until the vegetables are well dispersed through the meat. Using your hands or a small spoon, stuff this filling into the zucchini tubes, ensuring that the filling reaches right to the bottom. Lay the zucchini in a roasting pan and transfer to the oven for 30 minutes to bake.

Once baked, remove the zucchini from the pan and place on serving plates. Place the roasting pan over a low heat and add the white wine. Using a wooden spoon, deglaze the pan, scraping away any brown juices that have caramelized at its base. Continue to cook until the wine has almost evaporated, then add the veal stock and cook for 5–10 minutes, until slightly thickened.

Serve the zucchini hot with the veal sauce.

Escargots à la Bourguignonne

This classic French recipe is utterly delicious, though perhaps not for those who are watching their diet. Smothered in rich butter and punchy garlic, this will delight even the most cautious of diners.

Serves 4

24 large canned snails

24 large snail shells (optional)

For the garlic and parsley butter:

½ shallot, roughly chopped

3 garlic cloves, roughly chopped

1 bunch of parsley, leaves roughly chopped

1 tablespoon cognac

3½ oz (100 g) softened butter

salt and freshly ground black pepper

Preheat the oven to 400°F (200°C).

To make the butter, place the shallot, garlic, parsley and cognac in a blender and pulse until well combined. Add the butter to the blender and pulse again until well incorporated and bright green in color. Season with salt and pepper and set aside.

If using snail shells, stuff the snails into the shells and lay on a baking sheet. If not, divide the snails between 4 small individual ramekins on a baking sheet. Divide the butter between the snails, either spooning it into the shells or over the snails in the ramekins, ensuring that each snail is generously covered.

Transfer to the oven for 8 minutes, until the butter has melted and looks as if it has separated. Then, switch the oven to broil for a further 5 minutes, until the butter is bubbling and no longer looks separated.

Divide the snails between serving plates and serve with fresh bread alongside for dipping into the butter.

Caillettes d'Ardeche

These meatballs are fun and easy to prepare and make a wholesome winter dish. You can source the different pieces of pork from your butcher.

Serves 4–5

1 lb 7 oz (650 g) green Swiss chard leaves

2¾ oz (75 g) pork back fat

7 oz (200 g) pork neck

10½ oz (300 g) pork shoulder

2¾ oz (75 g) pork liver

7 oz (200 g) pork caul fat

4 garlic cloves, peeled

1 bunch of parsley, chopped

½ bunch of basil

1 thyme sprig

1 tablespoon + 1 teaspoon (20 g) fine salt

1 tablespoon (8 g) ground white pepper

1 dash of white wine

Preheat the oven to 300°F (150°C).

Blanch the chard in a pan of boiling salted water for 3 minutes, or until cooked. Drain and refresh in a bowl of iced water to keep those beautiful deep green colors.

Pass all the pork meat, including the back fat and liver, through a mincer together with the garlic and Swiss chard. Finely chop the fresh herbs and mix together with the minced meat. Season with the salt and pepper. With damp hands, divide the mixture equally into 4 or 5 balls depending on size. Rinse the pork caul fat under cold running water before laying out flat on a kitchen towel or paper towels. Tightly wrap each individual *caillette* with a single layer of the pork caul fat.

Place all the *caillettes* in a large ovenproof cast-iron frying pan or baking dish, drizzle the white wine over the top and bake in the oven for 30 minutes. Increase the oven temperature to 400°F (200°C), for the last 15 minutes until lightly colored and crispy on top. Serve immediately.

Broiled Sardines with a Parsley Crumb

These sardines are a perfect starter to any meal. They are also delicious cooked on the barbecue.

Serves 4 as a starter

4 cups (200 g) dried breadcrumbs

grated zest of 1 lemon

1 bunch of flat-leaf parsley, finely chopped

1 garlic clove, finely chopped

2 tablespoons olive oil, plus extra for drizzling

8 fresh whole sardines, scaled, gutted and butterflied

salt and freshly ground pepper

To serve:

toasted sourdough

fresh tomatoes

Stir the breadcrumbs, lemon zest, parsley and garlic together in a large bowl. Season to taste with salt and pepper.

Preheat the oven broiler to a medium-high heat. Brush a baking tray with a little olive oil and place the sardines, flesh-side down, onto the tray. Evenly distribute the breadcrumb mix all over the fish and place under the broiler for 5–10 minutes, depending on the size of the fish, until the breadcrumbs are nice and crisp and the flesh of the sardines are just cooked through.

These are best served with toasted sourdough and fresh tomatoes.

Rabbit with Mustard Relish

This is a modern take on the classic Lapin à la Moutarde *(see page 88) that retains many of the flavors of the original dish but makes for a much lighter meal.*

Serves 4

12 baby new potatoes

2 rabbit loins, each cut in half

2 rabbit racks, each cut in half

2 tablespoons olive oil

1½ tablespoons (20 g) butter

½ cup (125 ml) chicken stock

¼ cup (50 ml) dry white wine

3½ oz (100 g) green baby leaf salad

3½ oz (100 g) purple baby leaf salad

salt and freshly ground black pepper

1 tablespoon mustard seeds, toasted, to serve

For the mustard relish:

7 oz (200 g) mustard leaves or wild arugula leaves

1 anchovy in oil

1 pickled onion in white wine vinegar (see page 200)

1 teaspoon Dijon mustard

juice of ½ a lime

½ cup (100 ml) olive oil

Place the potatoes in a pan of salted water, bring to a boil and cook for about 8 minutes until tender. Drain and set aside to cool to room temperature.

To make the mustard relish, place all the ingredients in a blender and blend until smooth. Transfer to the fridge until ready to use.

Season both the loins and racks of rabbit with salt and pepper. Place 1 tablespoon of the olive oil in large frying or sauté pan over a medium heat. Once the oil is hot, add the rabbit to the pan and sear until it is nice and golden all over. Add the butter to the pan and baste the meat until it is caramelized and cooked through, around 12–14 minutes, depending on the size of your rabbit pieces. Transfer the rabbit to a board to rest, covered with aluminum foil. Deglaze the pan with the chicken stock and white wine and reduce for 5–10 minutes, until you obtain a light jus. Place the salad leaves in a bowl with the cooled potatoes and dress with the remaining olive oil and a tablespoon of the jus. Serve the rabbit drizzled with the remaining jus, the mustard relish and salad alongside and garnished with the toasted mustard seeds.

Roast Chicken, with Parsnip and Potato Mash

There are few things more comforting or simple than a roast chicken — it's a guaranteed crowd pleaser. Before it's even ready, the delicious smell wafting from the oven will have your family gathering in the kitchen and salivating.

Serves 4

1 whole chicken (approx. 3 lb 5 oz / 1.5 kg)

1 lemon, halved

2 garlic cloves, halved

1 thyme or rosemary sprig

3½ tablespoons (50 g) butter, softened

½ shallot, finely chopped

1¼ cup (300 ml) chicken stock

salt and freshly ground black pepper

For the mash:

1 lb 2 oz (500 g) potatoes, peeled and chopped into bite-sized pieces

14 oz (400 g) parsnips, peeled and chopped into bite-sized pieces

1 teaspoon salt

¾ cup (175 ml) whole milk, warmed

2 tablespoons (30 g) butter, cubed

2 tablespoons chopped chives

Preheat the oven to 400°F (200°C).

Remove the string from the chicken and stuff it with the lemon, garlic and herbs. Lay the chicken in a large roasting pan and, using your hands, rub the butter all over its skin. Season generously with salt and pepper and transfer to the oven to bake for around 50 minutes, until the juices run clear and the internal temperature of the meat is 150–160°F (65–70°C). Remove the lemon, garlic and herbs from the chicken and set aside in a medium pan to rest, covered, for at least 20 minutes.

While the chicken is cooling, prepare the mash. Place the potatoes and parsnips in a large pan and cover with water. Add the salt to the pan and place over a high heat. Once boiling, reduce the heat to a simmer and leave to cook for 20–25 minutes, until the vegetables are tender. Drain through a colander and return the vegetables to the pan. Using a potato masher, mash the vegetables to the consistency that you like, gradually adding the milk and butter as you go. Season to taste and transfer to a serving dish and scatter over the chives. Keep warm while you prepare the sauce.

Place the pan with the reserved lemon, garlic and herbs over a low heat and squeeze the lemons to release the juice. Discard the lemon halves and add the shallot to the pan. Cook for 5 minutes, until the shallots are softened, then add the chicken stock along with any juices that have oozed out of the chicken. Bring to a simmer and leave to cook for 5–10 minutes, until reduced by half and thickened.

Carve the chicken and serve with the mash and sauce alongside.

Butternut Pancakes

The butternut squash used in these pancakes imparts a delicious natural sweetness. These are perfect served as they are, but can be paired with a simple salad for a more substantial meal.

Serves 4

14 oz (400 g) butternut squash, peeled and seeds removed, roughly chopped

2 eggs

⅔ cup (125 ml) Greek yogurt

1¾ tablespoons (25 g) butter, melted

½ cup + 2 tablespoons (70 g) plain flour

1 pinch of ground nutmeg

1 tablespoon olive oil

salt and freshly ground black pepper

Preheat the oven to 325°F (160°C) and line a large baking sheet with parchment paper.

Lay the butternut squash out on the prepared baking sheet in a single layer and transfer to the oven to cook for 25 minutes, until tender. Once cooked through, transfer the pieces of squash to a large bowl and mash with a fork to obtain a rough purée.

In a separate bowl, whisk together the eggs, yogurt and melted butter until well combined. Add the butternut purée and sift in the flour. Add the nutmeg and season with salt and pepper, then whisk the mixture until well combined. Cover with plastic wrap and transfer to the fridge to rest for 30 minutes.

Once the mixture has rested, heat the oil in a frying pan over a medium heat. Once hot, pour a small ladleful of the mixture into the pan. Cook the pancake for 2 minutes, then flip and cook for 2 minutes more, until just golden brown. Keep warm while you make the remaining pancakes.

Serve the pancakes warm, paired with a simple salad, if desired.

Lapin à la Moutarde

This is a traditional braised rabbit recipe that is enjoyed by families all over France. The sauce is deliciously rich and creamy but is given a fiery punch by the combination of mustards used.

Serves 4

1 whole rabbit, jointed or unjointed

2 tablespoons wholegrain mustard

3½ tablespoons (50 g) butter

1 onion, finely chopped

1 carrot, peeled and diced into ½ inch (1 cm) cubes

100 g mushrooms, roughly chopped

1 garlic clove, crushed

1 thyme sprig

1 cup (250 ml) dry white wine

1¾ cup (400 ml) chicken stock

2 teaspoons Dijon mustard

½ + ⅓ cup (200 ml) whipping cream

½ bunch of flat-leaf parsley, leaves chopped

salt and freshly ground black pepper

If jointing your rabbit yourself, take the rabbit carcass and lay it on its back. Start by removing the hind legs with a sharp knife, following the hip joint. Next, make an incision between the rib cage and the saddle and dislocate one from the other with your hands. Finally, remove the front legs, slicing through the collar bone. You should be left with 6 joints of rabbit.

Preheat the oven to 325°F (160°C).

Place the rabbit pieces in a large bowl and smear with 1 tablespoon of the wholegrain mustard. Season with salt and pepper and set aside.

Place the butter in a large Dutch oven over a medium heat. Once it is melted and bubbling, add the pieces of rabbit and sear until just golden on all sides, then remove from the pan and set aside. In the same pan, add the onion, carrot, mushrooms, garlic and thyme sprig and cook, stirring continuously, for about 10 minutes, until the vegetables are just tender.

Deglaze the pan with the white wine and continue to cook until almost all of the alcohol has evaporated. Add the chicken stock, Dijon mustard and remaining wholegrain mustard, stir to combine, then return the rabbit pieces to the pan. Cover the pan with a lid and transfer to the oven to cook for about 25 minutes, until the rabbit is tender.

Pour the cream into the sauce, sprinkle over the chopped parsley and season to taste. Remove the pieces of rabbit from the pan and divide between serving plates, spooning over the sauce. Serve hot.

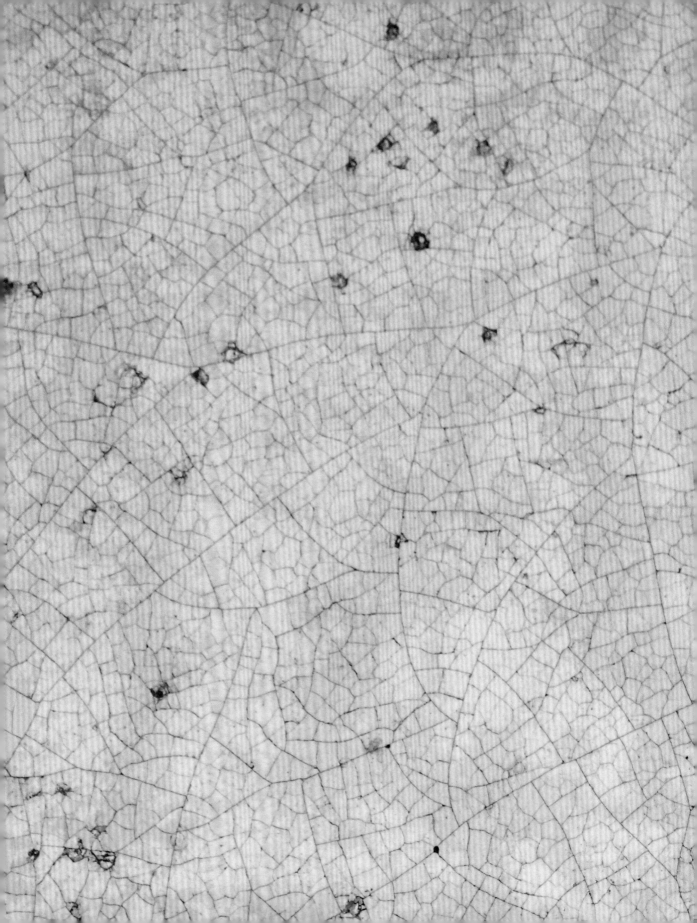

Feeding a crowd

Giselle

When family or friends are coming over we like to prepare as much of the food as possible in advance so we can enjoy ourselves with our guests. Many of these dishes are those that I ate as a child, such as *Pissaladière* (**see** page 98) and tarts. Both of these can be cut into bite-sized pieces and eaten as an appetizer to whet your appetite. We also make traditional southern French dips such as Tapenade and Anchoïade (**see** page 96), tripling the recipes for larger batches that will fill several jars and serving them with lots of crudités and good bread so that everyone can help themselves.

Another great treat is *petites fritures* — Deep-fried Whitebait with Tartar Sauce, which we all find irresistible (**see** page 114). And then there is our beautiful white pizza with a topping of bacon, white onion and Roquefort (**see** page 102) — not a tomato in sight. That also disappears extra fast.

All of the recipes in this chapter serve more than four people as part of a larger spread.

Spreads and Dips

These are probably the easiest recipes to feed a crowd with. Not only are they super-tasty snacks, they only take a couple of minutes to make and they are typically provincial. They are perfect served on grilled bread or simply used as a dipping sauce.

Anchoïade
makes 1 small jar, about 12 oz (350 g)

2¼ oz (60 g) jarred anchovy fillets

1 teaspoon small capers

1 garlic clove, peeled

1 teaspoon Dijon mustard

½ shallot, roughly chopped

1 tablespoon lemon juice

1 handful of parsley, chopped

1 pinch of freshly ground black pepper

4 tablespoons good-quality olive oil

Place all the ingredients, except the oil, in a small processor and blend for a few seconds before gently adding the oil in a steady stream until the sauce has emulsified and thickened. Store in a sealed sterilized jar in the fridge for up to 10 days.

Tapenade
makes 1 small jar, about 12 oz (350 g)

9 oz (250 g) pitted black olives

6 anchovy fillets

2 tablespoons small capers

1 garlic clove, peeled

½ cup (100 ml) olive oil

Place all the ingredients, except the oil, in a small food processor and blend together for a few seconds before gently adding the olive oil in a steady stream until thickened. Store in a sealed sterilized jar in the fridge for up to 10 days.

Brandade de Morue
Serves 6 as an aperitif

10½ oz (300 g) dried, salted stock fish fillets (unsalted fish, such as cod, which is air- and wind-dried on wooden racks)

⅔ cup (150 ml) warm milk

⅔ cup (150 ml) good-quality olive oil

freshly ground black pepper

Soak the fish for 48 hours in cold water, changing it every 12 hours. Once the time is completed, drain and place the fillets in a large saucepan and pour in enough fresh cold water to cover. Cook over a medium heat and, as soon as the water has reached boiling point, turn off the heat and leave the stock fish to poach for 10 minutes. Remove the fish from the pan and flake the flesh, making sure you remove any bones. Do not remove the skin, as this helps bind the spread.

For an authentic brandade, place the cooked fish in a mortar, add pepper to taste and grind with a pestle until it is a paste-like texture. Place in a cast-iron pan over a low heat and reheat, then while stirring vigorously, alternately pour in a little milk and olive oil. Continue until both liquids have been completely combined, without ever simmering or boiling. Leave to cool, then serve cold. Store in an airtight container in the fridge for 3–4 days.

Pissaladière

This is a typical southern French recipe, full of audacious flavors and perfect to slice into bite-sized morsels to feed guests.

Serves 4

2 tablespoons olive oil

2 lb 4 oz (1 kg) white onions (or 5 large pieces), finely sliced

¾ oz (20 g) chopped salted anchovies

1 oz (30 g) Anchoïade or Tapenade (see page 96)

1 thyme sprig

1 sheet of puff pastry (approx. 14 oz/400 g)

1 egg yolk mixed with 1 tablespoon milk to use as an egg wash

6 fresh or lightly smoked anchovies

freshly ground black pepper

green salad, to serve

Preheat the oven to 350°F (180°C).

Heat the oil in a large saucepan, then add the onions and sear over a high heat for at least 5 minutes, stirring constantly. Once the onions start to color and tenderize, reduce the heat and add the salted anchovies together with the Anchoïade or Tapenade and thyme. Cover the pan with a lid and leave the onions to cook gently for a further hour, stirring every 10 minutes. Once the onions have reduced by half and are a beautiful caramelized color, uncover and cook for another 10 minutes. All the moisture left in the saucepan will evaporate, leaving you with a delicious onion paste. Season with a pinch of pepper before leaving to cool completely.

Place the puff pastry on a baking tray and prick all over with a fork. Fold over the edges to create a crust and brush all over with the egg wash. Precook the puff pastry in the oven for 7 minutes (this ensures that it won't get a soggy base). Spread the onion mixture all over the part-cooked pastry, staying within the crust. Once again, brush the edges of the pastry with egg wash for extra shininess. Bake in the oven for 30 minutes, or until the pastry is golden brown and crisp.

Remove from the oven and scatter the fresh anchovies over the top. Best served lukewarm or cold with a lovely green salad.

Roast Onion, Fennel and Pesto Tart

Giselle: This recipe is a huge favorite of my family, especially my mother, who really enjoys eating this tart as a sophisticated appetizer.

Makes a 10 inch (25 cm) tart

2 tablespoons butter, plus a little extra for greasing

6 red onions, quartered

3 large fennel bulbs, halved

1 drizzle of olive oil

1 thyme sprig

1 tablespoon (15 g) superfine sugar

2 egg yolks, beaten, to make an egg wash

3 tablespoons basil pesto

¼ oz (10 g) toasted pine nuts

1½ tablespoons (10 g) Parmesan shavings

1 handful of basil leaves (optional)

salt and freshly ground black pepper

For the shortcrust pastry:

8 oz cup (225 g) plain flour, plus extra for dusting

1 teaspoon salt

1 oz (25 g) cold butter, cubed

1 oz (25 g) lard, cubed

2 tablespoons cold water

To make the pastry, sift the flour and salt into a large bowl. Add the butter and lard and rub together with your fingertips until the mixture resembles breadcrumbs. Pour in the water and bring the dough together in your hands; but do not overwork it. Leave to rest in the fridge for 30 minutes before using.

Preheat the oven to 350°F (180°C). Line a large baking tray with foil and grease a 10 inch (25 cm) tart pan with butter.

Place the chopped onions and fennel on the prepared baking tray and drizzle the oil over the top. Season with salt and pepper, add the thyme, then mix together. Bake in the oven for 25 minutes, or until the veggies start to brown on the edges but are not completely cooked. Keep the oven on.

Heat the butter in a large frying pan over a medium heat, then scatter the sugar into the pan. Throw in the vegetable chunks and mix around

for 2–3 minutes until they are coated with a light caramel, then remove from the pan and let cool.

Roll out the pastry on a lightly floured surface until ¼ inch (5 mm) thick and use to line the prepared tart pan. Press the pastry into place before trimming off any excess pastry around the edges. Prick the base of the tart with a fork and brush all over with the beaten egg yolks. Blind bake in the oven for 20 minutes, then remove the tart, remove the baking beans, and carefully take it out of the pan. Leave to cool until the pastry is cool enough to handle.

Spread the pesto evenly over the base of the tart, then elegantly place the roasted onions and fennel on top. Brush the rims again with the remaining egg wash and bake the tart in the oven for a further 10–15 minutes. Once all the vegetables are roasted and the pastry is brown, remove from the oven and sprinkle the pine nuts on top. Sprinkle the Parmesan on top while the tart is still warm and serve with basil leaves scattered over the top, if desired.

White Pizza with Lardons and Crème Fraîche

Tomato sauce-less pizzas are delicious; just be sure to pack in the bold flavors with the topping.

makes a 12 inch (30 cm) pizza

2 tablespoons olive oil

1 large white onion, finely sliced

1 teaspoon dried mixed herbs

7 oz (200 g) smoked bacon lardons

9 oz (250 g) Pizza Dough (**see** page 242)

plain flour, for dusting

½ cup (100 g) crème fraîche

1 oz (30 g) Roquefort cheese, cut into small pieces

salt and freshly ground black pepper

Line a large baking tray with parchment paper.

Heat the oil in a large saucepan over a medium heat. Add the sliced onions and cook for 5 minutes, stirring occasionally. Season with salt, pepper and the dried mixed herbs. Once the onions are tender, remove them from the pan and set aside on paper towels.

Dry-fry the lardons in a nonstick frying pan over a medium-high heat. Once they have rendered their water and begin to color, immediately remove them from the heat.

Roll out the pizza dough on a lightly floured surface to the size of the baking tray and slide it onto the prepared baking tray. Spread the crème fraîche over the dough and scatter the cooked lardons and onions on top. Bake in the oven for 15–20 minutes until brown and crispy on the outside. Remove from the oven and sprinkle the Roquefort all over to melt, and season with pepper.

Spinach and Goat Cheese Quiche

If you like goat cheese, this recipe is perfect for you. It is a crispy and creamy heavenliness.

makes a 10 inch (25 cm) quiche

1 tablespoon butter

2 garlic cloves, chopped

1 lb 5 oz (600 g) spinach leaves, tough stems removed

9 oz (250 g) rolled-out puff pastry

1 egg yolk mixed with 1 tablespoon milk to use as an egg wash

3 whole eggs

½ cup (100 ml) semi-skimmed milk (2.5%)

⅓ cup (80 ml) whipping cream

3½ oz (100 g) soft goat cheese, cut into 6 bite-sized pieces

salt and freshly ground black pepper

Heat the butter in a saucepan with the chopped garlic. When the garlic is beginning to brown after about 2 minutes, add the spinach leaves. Use a spatula to make sure all the leaves get coated in butter and garlic and season to taste with salt and pepper. Cover the pan with a lid and cook for 3 minutes until the spinach has completely wilted. Remove from the heat and drain. Firmly press the spinach in a colander with the back of a spoon to remove any excess water. Leave the cooked spinach to cool in the fridge for 2 hours before roughly chopping with a sharp knife.

Preheat the oven to 350°F (180°C).

Line a 10 inch (25 cm) quiche pan with the puff pastry, then brush the pastry with egg wash. Make a few little incisions with help of a fork and blind bake the puff pastry in the oven for 15 minutes to prevent the base going soggy. As soon as the pastry is lightly blond, remove from the oven, remove the baking beans, and evenly spread out the chopped spinach over the pastry.

Whisk the eggs, milk and whipping cream together in a medium bowl and season with salt and pepper. Pour the mixture over the spinach to cover (the mix will rise during cooking). Finally, scatter the goat cheese over the quiche and bake in the oven for 40 minutes until lovely and golden. Best served lukewarm or cold.

Meat Loaf

This is real sharing comfort food!

Serves 4

½ carrot, chopped

½ celery stick, chopped

2 white mushrooms, chopped

1 shallot, chopped

2 garlic cloves

1 handful of flat-leaf parsley leaves

1 lb (450 g) ground beef

3 tablespoons panko breadcrumbs

1 teaspoon dried thyme

2 teaspoons fine salt

1 pinch of ground nutmeg

1 pinch of dried red chili flakes

1 egg

2 tablespoons ketchup, plus a little extra for brushing

1 tablespoon Worcestershire sauce

Preheat the oven to 375°F (190°C).

Place the carrot, celery, mushroom and shallot together with the garlic and parsley in a small blender and lightly blend into small chunks; being careful not to purée the vegetables. Set aside.

Place the minced meat in a large bowl, add the breadcrumbs and thyme, then season with the salt, nutmeg and chili. In a separate smaller bowl, whisk the egg, ketchup and Worcestershire sauce together before adding to the minced meat. Finally, add the chopped veggies and gently fold into the meat.

Shape the mixture into a 8 inch (20 cm) long loaf, on a baking sheet lined with parchment paper, avoiding pressing and compacting the mixture, then brush a little ketchup on top of the meat loaf before baking. Alternatively, you can cook it in a loaf pan to keep its shape. Bake in the oven for approximately 30 minutes depending on the thickness of the minced meat, until it has a golden brown exterior and the center has reached 150°F (65°C).

Remove from the oven and leave to rest for 2 hours before attempting to slice. It is delicious served cold as finger food.

Spring Lamb Chops with Garlic and Mint Sauce

We don't eat a lot of meat but this particular sharing dish is always welcomed come spring.

Serves 4 as an aperitif

1 rack of spring lamb (with 8 bones), French trimmed

For the marinade:

4 tablespoons olive oil

1 rosemary sprig, leaves picked

1 thyme sprig, leaves picked

1 teaspoon *piment d'Espelette* or chili powder

1 teaspoon sea salt

For the sauce:

½ cup (100 ml) milk

2 garlic cloves, halved

1 cup (250 ml) rapeseed oil

1 tablespoon chopped mint

1 tablespoon chopped flat-leaf parsley

salt and freshly ground black pepper

For the marinade, place all the ingredients in a mortar and grind with a pestle until the oil is properly incorporated. Rub the marinade all over the lamb rack and leave in the fridge for 4 hours.

To make the sauce, place the milk and garlic in a small saucepan and gently heat making sure the liquid never boils. Once hot, use a hand-held blender to mix the garlic and milk together, then gradually incorporate the oil into the mixture until the sauce emulsifies and thickens. Season to taste, pour the sauce into a small bowl and leave to cool for 1 hour. Once completely cold, whisk the chopped herbs into the sauce.

Preheat the oven to 350°F (180°C).

Season the rack of lamb to taste with salt and pepper. Heat a large frying pan over a medium-high heat and brown the rack on the meaty sides for about 1–2 minutes, then turn over and color the other sides for a further 1 minute. Finally, brown the ends briefly so that all of the exposed meat is seared.

Place the rack in an appropriately sized roasting tray and roast in the oven for approximately 10 minutes depending on the size of the rack, or until the probe of a meat thermometer inserted into the core shows approximately 110°F (43°C). Leave the meat to rest for a further 5 minutes before slicing each chop and serving with the sauce.

Pommes Dauphines

These are a thousand times more delicious than fries. Make your own scrumptious pommes dauphines *to accompany your dipping sauces. It is best to make the mixture the day before.*

makes 30–40, depending on size

1 lb 12 oz (800 g) potatoes, peeled and quartered

1 teaspoon grated nutmeg

1 teaspoon fine salt

1 pinch of freshly ground black pepper

approx. 4 cups (1 liter) vegetable oil, for frying

For the choux pastry:

1¼ cup (120 g) plain flour

a good pinch of sea salt

1 cup (250 ml) whole or semi-skimmed milk

⅓ cup (90 g) butter

4 eggs

Place the potatoes in a saucepan filled with cold salted water and cook for 15–20 minutes until tender.

Meanwhile, it is important that you prepare the choux pastry in advance, as both elements must still be warm when they are mixed together.

Sift the flour and salt into bowl and set aside. Put the milk and butter in a medium saucepan over a medium heat and stir until the butter melts. Allow the mixture to come to a rolling boil, then immediately remove the pan from the heat. Add the flour and salt to the saucepan in one go and mix well with a wooden spoon until it all comes together as a dough. Reduce the heat to a minimum and keep stirring the dough energetically for a further 2 minutes (it's normal that the pastry starts sticking to the base

of the pan). Place the dough in a large bowl and vigorously beat the eggs in, one by one. You should have a smooth choux pastry. As soon as the potatoes are cooked, drain thoroughly and pass through a potato ricer. Weigh out 1 lb 2 oz (500 g) and add to the choux pastry. Mix well with a wooden spoon and season well with nutmeg, salt and pepper. Leave in the fridge overnight.

The next day, heat a deep-fryer or shallow pan with vegetable oil to 350°F (180°C).

Scoop out 1 tablespoon of the mix and gently add spoonfuls to the hot oil. Fry them for 2 minutes until golden brown and crispy, then remove with a slotted spoon and drain on paper towels. Serve.

Salmon Fish Cakes

We absolutely love this recipe — delicious fish cakes bursting with herby flavors.

makes 5 small fish cakes

5½ oz (150 g) salmon fillets, scaled and pin-boned

½ + ⅓ cup (200 ml) whole or semi-skimmed milk

1 thyme sprig

4½ oz (130 g) mashed potatoes (about 2 large potatoes)

1 tablespoon olive oil

1 egg

1 oz (30 g) breadcrumbs (either panko or regular)

⅛ oz (5 g) chopped cilantro

⅛ oz (5 g) chopped chives

finely grated zest of ½ a lime

4 tablespoons avocado or coconut oil, for frying

salt and freshly ground black pepper

For the coating:

about ¾ cup (75 g) plain flour

2 eggs

3½ oz (100 g) dried breadcrumbs

Place the fish in a saucepan and pour over the milk. Add a pinch of salt and the thyme before gently bringing to a boil. As soon as the first big bubbles appear turn off the heat and set aside. Once the milk is lukewarm remove the fish and flake the flesh. Set aside.

In a large bowl, add all the remaining ingredients in no particular order including the flaked salmon. Season to taste and mix together until combined, then leave to set in the fridge for 2 hours. Once chilled, divide the fish cake mixture into 5 portions, then shape and pat into circles about ¾ inch (2 cm) thick (as you would when making a burger).

All the ingredients needed for the coating must be put in individual shallow dishes. The eggs must be beaten and seasoned with a pinch of salt and pepper before using.

Bring the avocado oil to a medium heat or 350°F (180°C) in a large pan. Meanwhile, coat the fish cakes in the flour, shaking off the excess, then repeat the process with the beaten eggs, letting the excess drip off. Finally, dredge the fish cakes in breadcrumbs, turning twice and patting to adhere.

Pan-sear the fish cakes, in batches, for 2 minutes on each side until a caramelized brown color, then remove and drain on paper towels. Serve.

Deep-fried Whitebait with Tartar Sauce

We generally find these small fish at our local market. They are extremely easy to prepare and perfect to feed a hungry crowd. In French we call this recipe Petites Fritures.

Serves 4 as finger food

1 lb 2 oz (500 g) whitebait

1 teaspoon salt, plus a pinch

2¼ oz (65 g) plain flour

rapeseed or sunflower oil, for frying

For the tartar sauce:

1 large egg yolk

1 teaspoon Dijon mustard

2 tablespoons lemon juice

¼ pint (150 ml) sunflower or rapeseed oil

½ shallot, finely chopped

1 tablespoon chopped capers

1 tablespoon chopped pickles

1 handful of curly parsley, chopped

1 teaspoon white wine vinegar (optional)

salt and freshly ground black pepper

Heat the oil in a deep-fryer to 350°F (180°C).

For the sauce, place the egg yolk, mustard and 1 tablespoon of the lemon juice in a small bowl. While whisking, gradually incorporate half of the oil until the sauce thickens and emulsifies like a mayonnaise. Whisk in the remaining lemon juice and oil until combined. Rinse the shallot under cold water then add to the mayonnaise with the capers, pickles and chopped parsley and mix until combined. Season well with salt, pepper and the vinegar if needed.

Rinse the small fish under cold water making sure no impurities remain, then pat dry with paper towels before covering the fish with the 1 teaspoon salt and the flour. Use your hands to mix and fully coat the whitebait in the flour.

If you don't have a fryer, heat the oil in a deep frying pan to 350°F (180°C). Fry the fish in several batches for 3–5 minutes until golden brown and crispy. Remove with a slotted spoon and drain on paper towels. Sprinkle a pinch of salt on the whitebait as soon as you remove them from the pan and serve piping hot with the tartar sauce.

"Whitebait" refers to the immature fry of a fish, most commonly herring.

Wild Mushroom Bruschetta

Giselle: My siblings and I used to compete in "mushroom picking" as children, especially in spring when our favorite varieties were out.

Serves 4

10½ oz (300 g) wild mushrooms, such as St George, mousseron and oyster

2 tablespoons olive oil, plus extra for drizzling

1 shallot, finely chopped

1 tablespoon butter

1 garlic clove, halved

4 thick slices of sourdough bread

1 handful of watercress

1 oz (30 g) Parmesan shavings

salt and freshly ground black pepper

Brush any grit off the mushrooms and slice them until they are all the same size.

Heat the olive oil in a large frying pan and cook the mushrooms over a medium-high heat for 2 minutes until wilted. Add the shallot to the pan together with the butter and stir with a fork pricked with a garlic half. Season to taste with salt and pepper.

Remove the mushrooms from the pan once they are crisp and lightly browned.

Meanwhile, heat a chargrill pan over a medium-high heat. Brush the bread on both sides with a drizzle of oil, then toast on the chargrill for 2 minutes each side or until lightly charred. Rub one side with the remaining garlic clove.

Stir the watercress leaves into the mushroom mixture and immediately pile onto the toasted bread. Finish with the Parmesan shavings.

It is recommended that you do not forage for your own wild mushrooms, as there are many poisonous varieties that are very similar in appearance to edible varieties.

"Honeycomb" Zucchini Cannelloni

This baked dish is as visually appealing as it is tasty!

Serves 3–4 and fills a 8 inch (20 cm) round ovenproof dish

3 large zucchini (1 lb 2 oz / 500 g)

salt and freshly ground black pepper

For the lamb filling:

1 tablespoon olive oil

2 garlic cloves, finely chopped

1 shallot, finely chopped

7 oz (200 g) brown button mushrooms, chopped or pulsed several times in a blender

7 oz (200 g) minced lamb

1 tablespoon chopped thyme

5½ oz (150 g) spreadable soft goat cheese

For the béchamel:

1¼ oz (35 g) butter

1¼ oz (35 g) plain flour

9½ oz (280 ml) milk

1 oz (30 g) grated Beaufort or Gruyère cheese, plus a little extra for topping

2–3 pinches of ground nutmeg, to taste

For the filling, heat the olive oil in a frying pan over a medium heat. Add the garlic and shallots and sauté for 2 minutes until translucent. Add the chopped mushrooms and season well. Once the mushrooms have rendered all their water, transfer them to a bowl. Use the same frying pan to sauté the minced meat. Cook for 3–4 minutes until slightly colored and cooked through. Season with salt, pepper and thyme before adding to the bowl with the mushrooms. While still hot, incorporate the soft goat cheese. Once it is melted the mixture should have a perfectly moist texture. Set aside.

Finely slice the zucchini with a mandolin or a knife approximately ¼ inch (5 mm) thick. The zucchini strips must be thin enough to manipulate, but thick enough to remain stable in the dish. Bring a large pot of salted water to a boil and add all the zucchini strips. After 1½ minutes, drain the zucchini and immediately refresh in a bowl of ice-cold water. Make sure the strips are patted dry with paper towels before using. Roll up each zucchini strip and tightly place them in a 8 inch (20 cm) round ovenproof

dish to create a "honeycomb" bed of greenery. Fill three-quarters of each hole with the lamb filling, making sure you press the meat down to get enough in each zucchini.

Preheat the oven to 350°F (180°C).

To make the béchamel, place the butter in a medium saucepan and melt. Add the flour to the pan and whisk together until it is a thick homogenous paste (known as a "roux"). Gradually incorporate the milk, whisking constantly so no lumps form. Boil for 2 minutes until thick and glossy. Finally, add the cheese and season well with salt, pepper and nutmeg.

While the béchamel is still hot and malleable, delicately spoon over the remaining meat to top up the zucchini tubes. You should have a beautiful dish resembling honeycomb. Sprinkle with more cheese over the top and bake in the oven for 20–25 minutes until the béchamel has crisped and browned.

Truffled Camembert

The Ardèche is known for its fragrant truffles, so make sure to use them in your favorite dishes. The whole Roux family are cheese lovers, and on special occasions this particular recipe sits more than happily on the cheese board.

Serves 4

3½ oz (100 g) good-quality
   mascarpone

3 oz (80 g) cooked and peeled
   chestnuts

1¼ oz (35 g) fresh black truffle

1 Camembert cheese (9 oz / 250 g),
   chilled

salt and freshly ground black pepper

Whisk the mascarpone to a creamy consistency in a large bowl. Roughly chop the chestnuts and finely grate the truffle before adding both to the bowl. Mix and season to taste with salt and pepper.

Delicately slice the refrigerated Camembert cheese in half horizontally and spread the mascarpone mixture onto one side. Put the other half of the cheese on top to close, then wrap in plastic wrap. Leave in the refrigerator for 48 hours. For extra flavor and creaminess remember to take out the truffled cheese at least 2 hours before serving.

Spinach, Red Onion and Blue Cheese Bread Pudding

This is the ideal recipe when you have a few slices of stale bread in your cupboard. Economic, utterly delicious and an original twist on a classic dessert that everybody enjoys.

Serves 4

1 tablespoon butter, plus extra for greasing

4 red onions, finely sliced

2 tablespoons cider vinegar

1 lb 2 oz (500 g) spinach

1 garlic clove, smashed with the palm of your hand

2 tablespoons Dijon grain mustard

2 eggs

7 oz (200 ml) whole milk

3½ oz (100 g) crème fraîche

1 pinch of ground nutmeg

7–8 slices of bloomer bread

2¾ oz (75 g) blue cheese, such as Stilton

salt and freshly ground black pepper

Preheat the oven to 350°F (180°C), and grease a 8½ inch (22 cm) round cake pan with butter.

Heat ½ tablespoon of the butter in a large frying pan over a medium-high heat before adding the onions. Once they have rendered all their water, deglaze with the cider vinegar and reduce the heat. Cook the onions for 15–20 minutes, stirring occasionally, until soft and a beautiful caramel color. Season to taste with salt and pepper and leave to cool.

Cut off the thick stems of the spinach and thoroughly rinse the leaves under cold running water to remove any sand or dirt. Drain and place in a salad spinner to remove any excess water.

Heat the remaining butter in a large frying pan over a medium-high heat. Add the crushed garlic to the pan followed by the spinach and sauté for 3 minutes until the spinach is completely wilted and there is no liquid left in the pan. Season to taste,

then remove and discard the garlic and take the pan off the heat.

Whisk the mustard and eggs together in a large bowl. Gradually pour in the milk and crème fraîche, then season with salt, pepper and nutmeg. Place the sliced bread into the egg mixture and leave for 2 minutes to absorb enough liquid without going soggy and unmalleable.

Delicately fill the base of your greased mold by arranging 2 large slices of bread on the bottom. Place the cooked spinach, onions and remaining bread on top, then pour any of the remaining liquid mixture into the dish to fill all the little nooks and crannies. Finally, crumble over the blue cheese and bake in the oven for 15–20 minutes until golden brown and crispy. Serve.

Today's Trends

Emily

I've been lucky as I have grown up around good food, traveled to many countries and eaten in so many nice places. I have also worked in some amazing restaurants and now I'm developing my own style of cooking. I'm interested in the trends of today but I like to use them in the way that I want to eat. I like lighter food than the traditional French style. My aim is to take the trends but make them yummier while keeping the food healthy. I love ingredients like kale, sprouting broccoli, red rice and avocado, all of which are so good for you but also delicious. I don't drink coffee but I find it very interesting to cook with as I love the flavor.

I wasn't really aware of all these food trends when I was working in Paris — the French are just not into them like we are in Britain. But when I came home I found that mum had things like quinoa and coconut flour in her cupboard — she's always been keen on the latest ideas and on healthy ingredients — and I began to cook with them. The recipes I've come up with take a modern approach. They don't contain much fat or sugar, and there are few sauces, but there is lots of flavor. I enjoy reinterpreting classic French techniques in a way that appeals to younger people today, and working with unusual ingredients, such as kabocha squash and chia seeds. I also like to experiment with gluten-free dishes and everyone enjoys the recipe for Gluten- and Dairy-free Blueberry and Hazelnut Muffins (see page 130) that mom shared with me.

Dairy-free Avocado Mousse and Gluten-free Granola

Emily: Avocado is a huge favorite of mine; I use it as much in sweet as in savory dishes. This is a really simple recipe that you can rustle up when there is a ripe avocado left in the fridge. Eat this dessert as is just like yogurt, although, adding a little crunch with the granola makes it even yummier.

Mousse serves 3 and Granola serves 4–6

For the granola:

9 oz (250 g) gluten-free oats

2¼ oz (60 g) sunflower seeds

2¼ oz (60 g) pumpkin seeds

2 tablespoons linseeds

2¼ oz (60 g) hazelnuts, roughly chopped

1½ oz (40 g) flaked almonds

1 tablespoon coconut oil

2¼ oz (65 g) peanut butter

2¼ oz (60 g) honey

3 tablespoons maple syrup

2¼ oz (65 g) raisins

2¼ oz (65 g) goji berries

For the mousse:

2 avocados

1½ oz (40 g) unsweetened coconut milk or almond milk

1½ oz (40 g) honey

1 vanilla pod, scraped

2 tablespoons lemon juice

Preheat the oven to 250°F (120°C), and line a baking tray with parchment paper.

Mix the oats, seeds and nuts together in a large bowl.

Place the oil, peanut butter, honey and maple syrup in a small saucepan and gently heat. Once all the ingredients are properly combined and melted pour over the dry mix. Make sure all the oats and nuts are coated before spreading out on the prepared baking tray. Bake in the oven for 1½ hours until beautifully golden brown, making sure to mix and break up the pieces halfway through cooking. Remove from the oven and incorporate the dried fruit. Leave to cool.

To make the mousse, mix all the ingredients together in a food processor until silky smooth. Sprinkle the granola on top and eat right away as the avocado has a tendency to discolor.

127

Black Chia Porridge with Bamboo Crunch

Chia seeds are trendy nowadays with their numerous health benefits, although they can be a little bland if not prepared properly and accompanied with the right ingredients. If you are always in a hurry in the morning, this super-healthy porridge pot is the answer. You can prepare a few batches in advance and add different toppings as you go.

Fills a 4 oz (125 ml) jar

For the porridge:

2½ oz (70 g) blackberries, plus extra
    for the topping

3½ oz (100 ml) unsweetened
    almond milk

1 tablespoon lemon juice

1 tablespoon honey

1¾ oz (50 g) chia seeds

For the bamboo crunch:

1½ oz (42 g) demerara (raw) sugar

2¾ oz (75 g) plain flour

1 pinch of salt

¼ oz (12 g) ground bamboo charcoal
    (optional, buy online or from
    health-food stores)

1¾ oz (50 g) soft butter

To make the porridge, place all the ingredients, except the chia seeds, in a small food processor and blend until it is a beautiful dark purple color. Pour the mixture into a small jar and mix in the chia seeds. Leave in the fridge overnight to let the chia seeds swell up and double in size.

Preheat the oven to 350°F (180°C), and line a baking tray with parchment paper.

For the bamboo crunch, mix the sugar, flour, salt and charcoal together in a medium bowl. Add the butter and rub it into the flour mix using your fingertips until it resembles large crumbs. Evenly spread the crumbs out on the prepared baking tray and bake in the oven for 15 minutes. Don't forget them as you won't be able to judge on color. Remove from the oven and leave to cool and crunch up. If making ahead of time store in an airtight container for up to 3 days.

The next morning, scatter fresh blackberries on top of the porridge together with a few crunchy bites before devouring.

Gluten- and Dairy-free Blueberry and Hazelnut Muffins

Giselle: Michel and Emily usually find that gluten-free desserts don't quite satisfy them. However, this recipe has everybody's thumbs up!

Makes about 12 large muffins

4¼ oz (120 g) coconut flour

1 teaspoon baking soda

½ teaspoon salt

7 oz (200 g) honey

7 oz (200 g) coconut milk

6 eggs

4 tablespoons melted coconut oil, plus a little extra for greasing

1 tablespoon vanilla extract

1 oz (25 g) chia seeds

1¾ oz (50 g) fresh blueberries

1¾ oz (50 g) hazelnuts, roughly chopped

Preheat the oven to 365°F (185°C), and lightly oil a 12-hole muffin tray.

Whisk the flour, baking soda and salt together in a large bowl with a balloon whisk.

In a separate bowl, or blender, whisk the honey, milk, eggs, coconut oil and vanilla extract. Once everything is thoroughly combined pour over the dry mix and stir together until mixed. Finally, stir in the chia seeds, blueberries and hazelnuts. Stir for 2 minutes, as the chia seeds will absorb some of the moisture.

Fill the muffin pan to just under the rim with the batter and bake in the oven for 20–25 minutes until golden brown and slightly risen. Leave to cool slightly before serving.

Grilled Cobia, Garden Peas, Radishes and Black Butter

Cobia is the new farmed sustainable fish on the market. Its firm white flesh is perfect for grilling, but if you can't find it use cod instead.

Serves 4

½ tablespoon butter

9 oz (250 g) garden peas

1 green onion, finely sliced

17 oz (480 g) cobia or cod fillets (about 4 fillets)

olive oil, for drizzling

salt and freshly ground black pepper

microherbs, to garnish (optional)

For the black butter:

3½ oz (100 ml) white wine vinegar

4 oz (130 ml) white wine

2 shallots, roughly chopped

4½ oz (130 g) butter, cubed

2 sachets of squid ink

For the roasted radishes:

2 bunches of colored radishes, halved or quartered so they are all the same size (reserve 1 or 2 raw)

1 tablespoon honey

2 tablespoons olive oil

1 tablespoon lemon juice

Preheat the oven to 425°F (220°C).

To prepare the black butter, place the vinegar, wine and shallots in a medium saucepan and bring to a simmer. Cook for approximately 15 minutes, or until the shallots are tender and the liquid has reduced by two-thirds. Add the liquid and cooked shallots to a blender while still hot and blend to a smooth paste. With the machine on, gradually add the cubed butter and squid ink, then season the glossy and thickened sauce.

For the roasted radishes, place the radishes in a large bowl together with the honey, olive oil, lemon juice and seasoning. Once all the radishes are properly coated, scatter them on a baking sheet and roast in the oven for 15–20 minutes, stirring frequently.

Heat the butter in a medium saucepan, add the fresh peas and sauté and season the peas for 2 minutes before adding the green onion. Cover with a lid and cook for 5 minutes, or until the peas are tender.

Heat a griddle pan or barbecue to a medium-high heat. Season the cobia fillets with salt and pepper and drizzle a little olive oil on top. This fatty fish is best served pink, so depending on the size and thickness of the fish, cooking for 2 minutes on each side will suffice.

To serve, smear a tablespoon of the black butter on one side of each plate and place a grilled fish fillet on top. Arrange the peas and radishes elegantly on the side and garnish with microherbs, if liked.

Roasted Kale with Cannellini Beans and Chorizo

Although kale is super-trendy, it is difficult to drink the veggies raw in juice! It's much better to cook them in a tasty ragout.

Serves 3

2½ oz (70 g) kale leaves, roughly chopped

2 tablespoons olive oil

finely grated zest of 1 lemon

6 oz (175 g) cooking Spanish chorizo

2 small white onions (approx. 2¼ oz / 65 g), sliced

2 garlic cloves, sliced

4½ oz (125 g) cherry tomatoes, quartered

8½ oz (240 g) cannellini beans, drained and rinsed

1 sprig thyme

1 cup (250 ml) water

salt and freshly ground black pepper

Preheat the oven to 250°F (120°C), and line a large baking tray with parchment paper.

Place the kale in a large bowl, add the oil and salt and pepper, toss the kale until it is lightly coated all over, then spread it out on the prepared baking tray. Bake in the oven for about 20 minutes, or until a little crispy on the edges but still tender in the middle. Remove from the oven and sprinkle with lemon zest. Set aside.

Cut the chorizo into large diagonal slices, about ¾ inch (2 cm) wide and sear in a large nonstick frying pan over a medium-high heat for 3 minutes on each side (no fat needed), until lightly colored. Once cooked, remove the chorizo from the pan and set aside on paper towels. Use the fat left in the pan to sear the sliced onions and garlic for 3 minutes until tender, before adding the tomatoes

to the pan. Gently stir and cook for a further 5 minutes until the tomatoes have softened. Finally, add the cannellini beans, thyme and measured water, then reduce the heat to a gentle simmer and cook for a further 7 minutes.

Season to taste and remember to discard the sprig of thyme before serving with the roasted kale.

"Cooking" chorizo is unsmoked (soft) chorizo.

Individual Summer Tartelettes with a Quinoa Crust

These little tartelettes are ideal for people who have a wheat intolerance. The combinations of fruit and veggies you can use are endless.

Makes 5 tartelettes each 4 inches (10 cm) wide

For the quinoa crust:

rapeseed or sunflower oil, for greasing

10½ oz (300 g) quinoa

1 egg, beaten

salt and freshly ground black pepper

For the filling:

5 eggs

5¾ oz (160 g) peas

1 tablespoon butter

1 green onion, finely sliced

1 small red chili, finely sliced (optional)

5½ oz (150 g) baby spinach

1 tablespoon finely chopped mint leaves

1 handful of Tomberry tomatoes, halved or small cherry tomatoes, quartered

3 oz (80 g) feta

microherbs, mint leaves and beet cress, to garnish (optional)

Preheat the oven to 350°F (180°C), and grease 5 tartelette pans, 4 inches (10 cm) wide, with oil.

Cook the quinoa as you usually would in either water or vegetable stock (*see* page 49). Drain well and leave to cool in a bowl to room temperature. When the quinoa is at room temperature, incorporate the beaten egg and season with salt and pepper. The quinoa should no longer be crumbly but rather compact and holding itself together. At this point, start filling the prepared tartelette pans by gently pressing the mixture into place. The crust must be at least ¼ inch (5 mm) thick for it to hold during cooking.

Place the tartelettes in the oven for 12 minutes. Crack an egg into each small tart and return to the oven for a further 5 minutes. Once the egg is completely cooked, remove the tartelettes from the oven and leave to cool for a few minutes before carefully removing the crusts from the pans.

Meanwhile, blanch the peas for 1 minute in a pan of boiling salted water before refreshing in ice-cold water. Set aside.

Place the butter in a medium saucepan over a gentle heat. Add the green onion, peas and chili and sauté for 2 minutes. Remove from the heat, scatter in the spinach leaves and chopped mint and season well. Arrange the beautiful veggies all around the yolk and add the halved tomatoes and cheese for an extra tang. Garnish with a mixture of microherbs, mint leaves and beet cress, if liked, and serve immediately.

Pork Loin, Carrot "Spaghetti," Roast Parsnip and Cilantro Condiment

This original recipe is full of bold and fragrant flavors that tantalize your taste buds. The combination of Moroccan spice with the freshness of cilantro and lime juice brings the whole dish together.

Serves 4

1 lb 5 oz (600 g) pork loin

1 tablespoon olive oil

salt and freshly ground black pepper

For the cilantro condiment:

2 bunches of cilantro

2 tablespoons lime juice

4 tablespoons olive oil

1 teaspoon Dijon mustard

1 ice cube

For the garnish:

4 small parsnips, unpeeled but thoroughly washed

1 tablespoon honey

2 tablespoons olive oil

2 carrots, spiralized or cut into ribbons with a vegetable peeler

1 pinch of *ras el hanout*

2 tablespoons lemon juice

1 handful of mint cress or sliced mint leaves

Preheat the oven to 350°F (180°C).

Cut the pork into 4 even pieces and season with salt and pepper on each side. Heat the oil in large frying pan over a medium heat. Sear each side for 4–5 minutes, depending on the thickness of the meat until a lovely caramelized color. Set aside.

To make the condiment, blend all the ingredients together in a small food processor. Once all the ingredients are properly combined and it is a smooth paste, season with a pinch of salt. Store in the fridge until ready to use.

To prepare the garnish, place the parsnips on a baking tray together with the honey and 1 tablespoon of the olive oil. Mix together to coat the parsnips, then season with salt and pepper. Bake in the oven for 15–20 minutes, depending on the size of your veggies, until golden brown.

Meanwhile, heat 1 tablespoon of the olive oil in a large frying pan over a high heat. Place the spiralized carrots into the sizzling pan and sprinkle them with the *ras el hanout*. The carrots will cook very rapidly, so stir them constantly until they have softened but still remain *al dente*. Deglaze them with the lemon juice and season to taste with salt and pepper.

To serve, place a dash of cilantro condiment on the side of the plate with a small spatula or spoon. Intertwine a small nest of carrot "spaghetti" and place the parsnip next to it. Finally, add the pork, crispy side up, and garnish with mint cress over the top. Eat the carrot swirled around your fork (as you would real spaghetti).

Ras el hanout (translated as "top-shelf") is a Morrocan spice mixture made of anywhere from 10 to 100 different spices!

Whole Roasted and Spiced Cauliflower

This is an extremely easy recipe and perfect for a quick, light lunch. It's also a great vegetable accompaniment to Christmas lunch! You can always use the delicious yogurt topping to enlighten other dishes during the week.

Serves 4–6

5½ oz (150 g) Greek yogurt

finely grated zest and juice of 1 lemon

2 teaspoons smoked salt

1 tablespoon finely chopped garlic

1 tablespoon smoked paprika

1 teaspoon ground cumin

1 pinch of freshly ground black pepper

1 pinch of ground nutmeg

1 head cauliflower

good-quality olive oil, for drizzling

Preheat the oven to 400°F (200°C), and line a baking tray with parchment paper.

Whisk all the ingredients, except the cauliflower and olive oil, together in a large bowl. Dunk the whole cauliflower into the bowl and smear the marinade all over, then place it on the prepared baking tray. Bake in the oven for 45–60 minutes, or until the marinade has formed a beautifully colored crust.

It is best served lukewarm with a drizzle of good-quality olive oil. If you have any remaining marinade sauce, then keep it to serve with any fish or meat.

Spelt "Risotto," Sprouting Broccoli and Porcini

Spelt is a fantastic alternative to rice; it has a slightly nutty flavor and is very easily digested, especially for people who have difficulty digesting gluten. It also gives a warming and heartier feel to many dishes. Spelt is extremely versatile and can be used in many different ways. Here, spelt is used to make a wintery "risotto," but it can be made into biscuits, breads and is also a great supplement to salads.

Serves 4

4 cups (1 liter) vegetable stock or water

3 tablespoons olive oil

1 white onion, finely diced

7 oz (200 g) pearled spelt

4 oz (125 ml) white wine (optional)

2 tablespoons butter

3½ oz (100 g) Parmesan, grated

7 oz (200 g) sprouting broccoli, halved

7 oz (200 g) porcini, or any other mushroom that you like

1 garlic clove, crushed

1 green onion, sliced

Heat the stock or water in a pan and keep at a gentle simmer. When making this dish it is very important to keep the stock simmering at all times, otherwise you may interrupt the cooking process.

Heat 1 tablespoon of the oil in a large saucepan over a medium heat. Add the diced onion and cook for 2–3 minutes until softened and just beginning to color. Gradually add the spelt to the pan and stir well for 1 minute. Once the grains have absorbed all the moisture in the saucepan, deglaze the pan with the white wine and reduce the heat. Again, you must stir gently until all the alcohol has evaporated before adding more liquid.

Add 1 ladle of hot stock to the spelt and stir gently. Let the spelt absorb the stock before adding the next ladle. This slow method keeps the grain firm and concentrates the flavor of the dish. Repeat this process until the spelt is *al dente* —

cooked, yet still with a little bite. This should take about 40–45 minutes. When you feel the spelt has got the right texture briskly stir in the butter and Parmesan. You should have a perfect glossy finish.

Blanch the sprouting broccoli in a pan of boiling salted water for 2 minutes. Drain and set aside.

If necessary, cut the mushrooms to a similar size. In a large frying pan, heat the remaining olive oil over a medium-high heat. Add the mushrooms together with the garlic and toss them around so that they cook evenly for 2 minutes, or until the mushrooms have lightly browned. Add the sprouting broccoli and season to taste with salt and pepper.

Serve the "risotto" with the broccoli and mushroom mixture, then sprinkle the green onions all over the plate and devour.

Whole Grilled Squid with Red Rice and Fresh Herbs

Squid is a great sustainable fish option that is easy to cook in seconds. This recipe is amazing if you have an outside barbecue and it's the kind of dish that the whole Roux clan loves eating when in the south of France. Obviously, a griddle pan will also do the trick and taste just as fantastic!

Serves 4

4 (small–medium) whole squid, cleaned

10½ oz (300 g) red rice

3 cups (750 ml) water

3 tablespoons olive oil, for drizzling

¾ oz (20 g) mixed fresh herbs, such as tarragon, dill, cilantro, parsley

salt and freshly ground black pepper

For the marinade:

2 red chilies, deseeded and roughly chopped

½ stick of lemongrass, roughly chopped

grated zest and juice of 1 lemon, plus extra grated zest to garnish

1 tablespoon soy sauce

4 tablespoons olive oil

1 garlic clove, crushed

1 handful of mint leaves, finely sliced

To make the marinade, place the chilies and lemongrass in a large bowl together with the lemon juice and zest, soy sauce, olive oil and crushed garlic.

Wipe the squid with a dry cloth or paper towels to remove any remaining impurities, then place them in the bowl and rub the marinade all over. Sprinkle the mint leaves over the top of the squid with a couple of pinches of pepper. Cover with plastic wrap and leave in the fridge for at least 1 hour.

Meanwhile, rinse the red rice under cold water before putting it in a medium saucepan filled with the measured water and a pinch of salt. Once boiling, reduce the heat and leave the rice to simmer covered with a lid for 40–45 minutes. Once cooked, drain the rice, place the rice in a bowl and drizzle the olive oil over the top. Remove the squid from the marinade without discarding any excess oil or garnish inside. This will season and avoid the seafood sticking to the pan. Heat a griddle pan as hot as possible to get those special charred marks on the squid without overcooking them. Cook for 2 minutes on each side until beautifully tender.

Rinse your freshly plucked herbs under cold water and gently dry them off on a piece of paper. These little leaves add freshness and an extra crunch to the dish. Serve the squid with the herbs and extra grated lime zest over the top.

Lobster Ravioli with a Parsley Condiment and Bisque Sauce

Emily: I absolutely love lobster. It is such a special ingredient, but is only eaten on rare occasions and celebrations. I always savor every single bite.

Serves 6 as a starter and 4 as a main course

2 lb 4 oz (1 kg) lobster or 1 lb 5 oz (2 × 600 g) lobsters

2 tablespoons olive oil

1 shallot, finely chopped

¼ bunch of flat-leaf parsley, finely chopped

1 drop of Tabasco sauce

sea salt and freshly ground black pepper

For the pasta dough:

10½ oz (300 g) "00" flour, plus extra for dusting

a generous pinch of salt

5½ oz (150 g) egg yolk (or 7 yolks)

1 tablespoon water (optional)

For the bisque:

1 tablespoon olive oil

2 tablespoons butter

1 celery stick, roughly chopped

½ shallot, roughly chopped

1 garlic clove, crushed

2 tomatoes, chopped

2 tablespoons cognac

2 cups (500 ml) fish stock or water

For the condiment:

1 bunch of flat-leaf parsley

1 salted anchovy

1 teaspoon white wine vinegar

2 tablespoons olive oil

First, make the pasta dough. Place the flour, salt and egg yolks in a large bowl and mix together by hand until it is an elastic dough. You may need to add 1 tablespoon water to help knead the dough properly. Wrap the dough in plastic wrap and leave to rest in the fridge overnight.

The next day, prepare the lobster. Fill a large casserole dish with water and sea salt. Bring the water to a rolling boil. Kill the lobster instantly by putting a knife straight through its head. Leave the rubber bands on the pincers of the lobster until just before you submerge them in the pot. Place the lobster into the water head first, cover with a lid and cook for 8 minutes for a 2 lb 4 oz (1 kg) lobster or 6 minutes for 1 lb 5 oz (2 × 600 g) lobsters, until the lobster is bright red and has

firmed up. Remove from the heat and leave to cool in a bowl of ice-cold water, then remove the shell in 3 sections: the tail, the knuckles and the claws. Leave the tail to one side with a wet cloth on top to keep in the moisture. Keep all the carcasses to make the bisque. Shred the claw and knuckle meat for the ravioli filling and set aside.

Heat 1 tablespoon of the oil in a pan, add the shallot and cook until tender. Remove from the heat and leave to cool, then place it in a mixing bowl with the shredded claw meat and the finely chopped parsley. Season to taste with salt, pepper and the Tabasco and combine with the remaining oil. Using the palm of your hands, roll out the mixture into small balls, about ¾ inch (2 cm) wide. Leave in the fridge until the pasta dough is rolled out.

Continues next page...

Lobster Ravioli **continued**

Roll out the chilled pasta dough as finely as you possibly can on a lightly floured surface. It is much easier to use a pasta roller if you have one. The dough will fight you and bounce back but continue until it is $1/16$ inch (2 mm) thick. Once you have a long strip of pasta dough, place the balls of filling spaced every $2\frac{1}{2}$–$3\frac{1}{4}$ inches (6–8 cm) apart. Cut out squares around the fillings and brush the pasta dough with a little water before folding over diagonally. Tightly seal the opposite corners of each pasta square with your fingers, then, with the point of the triangle facing you, bring the other 2 edges together in a circle and press them together to form the ravioli shape.

For the bisque, smash the lobster carcasses with the back of a pan until they are small pieces. Heat the oil in a large saucepan over a medium heat and sear the lobster pieces for 4 minutes. Add the butter and roast the carcasses until the butter is foamy. Add the celery, shallot and garlic. When the vegetables are tender, incorporate the diced tomatoes. Deglaze the pan with the cognac and add the fish stock. Simmer for 25 minutes. Strain the bisque, making sure to get the maximum amount of juices from the lobster carcasses. You might need to reduce the bisque for a further 5 minutes to get the right consistency.

For the condiment, place the parsley, anchovy, vinegar and oil in a small blender and season to taste, then blitz well until it is a paste.

Cook the ravioli in a pan of boiling salted water for 3 minutes before draining carefully. Slice the lobster tail into $\frac{3}{4}$ inch (2 cm) slices and, if required, reheat it in the bisque making sure not to overcook it. Serve 3 or 4 ravioli on each serving plate, accompanied with 1 tablespoon of the condiment and 1 tablespoon of the bisque.

International
Influences

Emily

I've always enjoyed different kinds of food — Japanese, Italian, Chinese, South-east Asian — but Chinese is probably my very favorite. French food, of course, is known all around the world and that is usually what the French stick to. It seems to me that so many Japanese chefs in Paris cook French food — why not Japanese? England is so different. Here we embrace other cuisines and do them well. Paris is trying but London is way ahead.

All three of us love traveling and trying different cuisines. And it's so easy now to cook them at home. We can buy almost any ingredient we want — online if not in stores — so why shut yourself off from that? But at the same time we don't want to lose sight of our French roots.

I've learned so much from traveling and working in different countries and I have picked up lots of techniques and manners of cooking that I like to use in my own way. My repertoire ranges from Italian dishes, such as ravioles and risotto to Thai curries and Vietnamese spring rolls. I learned to love seaweed when working in Japan and have made a Japanese-inspired seaweed salad with crayfish tails (see page 169).

Risotto alla Milanese

This saffron-infused risotto is the pride of Milan.

Serves 6 as a "primi" or starter

9 oz (250 g) bone marrow (this includes the weight of the bone)

8½ cups (2 liters) chicken stock

2 tablespoons olive oil

1 white onion, finely chopped (into pieces the size of a grain of rice)

9 oz (250 g) Carnaroli rice

3½ oz (100 ml) white wine

1 pinch of saffron threads

2¼ oz (60 g) Parmesan, finely grated

1¼ oz (35 g) cold butter, cubed

salt and freshly ground black pepper

Preheat the oven to 250°F (120°C).

Place the whole bone marrow in a large ovenproof dish and cover with cold water. Add 1 teaspoon salt and bake in the oven for 3 hours. After the time has elapsed, remove the dish from the heat and leave to cool until you can remove the bone from the liquid with your hands. Do not discard the broth (it's delicious); simply add it to the chicken stock. Scoop out the marrow from the bone and cut into small cubes.

Place the chicken stock and cooking broth in a large saucepan and bring to a gentle simmer. Skim the top with a slotted spoon to remove any impurities.

Heat the olive oil in a large saucepan over a medium heat. Add the chopped onion and cook for 3–4 minutes until tender, but not colored. Add the diced bone marrow followed by the rice and toast the rice for 3 minutes until all the fat has been absorbed by the starch. Season with a pinch of salt and pepper, then deglaze the pan with the white wine and keep stirring with a wooden spatula until all the alcohol has evaporated. At this point, reduce the heat to a gentle simmer and add the first ladleful of stock. Risotto cooks for approximately 17 minutes, so keep feeding the rice with ladles of stock and stirring occasionally. After 15 minutes, add the saffron to the pan. The rice should have doubled in volume and absorbed nearly all of the liquid.

In the last remaining minutes sprinkle the Parmesan and butter into the pan and stir vigorously. Risotto should not be dry, so don't be afraid of adding an extra ladle of stock if needed. Check for seasoning before serving.

Warm Thai Noodle Salad with Seared Beef and Peanuts

This Thai-inspired noodle salad is the perfect dish to feed a large hungry family.

Serves 4

9 oz (250 g) thick rice noodles

1 tablespoon rapeseed oil

9 oz (250 g) rump steak

4 baby sweetcorn, halved

½ carrot, sliced into julienne (similar to matchsticks)

½ cucumber, sliced into julienne

2 oz (45 g) soybeans (edamame)

1 oz (25 g) peanuts, crushed

10 large mint leaves, finely sliced

1 tablespoon black sesame seeds

1 green onion, finely sliced

1 handful of cilantro leaves

For the dressing:

½ inch (1 cm) piece of fresh root ginger, peeled and grated

½ garlic clove, grated

1 small red chili, deseeded and finely sliced

4 tablespoons soy sauce

2 tablespoons sesame oil

2 tablespoons lemon juice

1 tablespoon fish sauce

Soak the noodles in a large bowl of boiling water until soft, then drain and leave to cool with the rapeseed oil added to the noodles to prevent them sticking together.

To prepare the dressing, simply whisk all the ingredients together in a small bowl until everything is well combined. Set aside.

Heat a griddle pan over a medium-high heat. Brush the beef with a little of the dressing and sear for 2½ minutes on each side, depending on the thickness, for a pink center. Remove from the pan and leave to rest and cool. Repeat with the baby sweetcorns, cooking them for 4–5 minutes until they are a beautiful charred color. Set aside.

Once the noodles are lukewarm place them in a large bowl. Mix in the sliced vegetables, soybeans and baby sweetcorn, then pour the dressing over the top and combine together with the peanuts and mint leaves. Finely slice the meat while still warm and incorporate into the salad.

Serve with a sprinkle of sesame seeds, green onion and cilantro leaves.

161

Vitello Tonnato

This is another Italian favorite. This cold starter always gets everybody's thumbs up!

Serves 4

1 lb 2 oz (500 g) loin of veal

1 egg yolk

1 tablespoon Dijon mustard

1 tablespoon white wine vinegar

7 oz (200 ml) neutral oil, such as rapeseed or sunflower

5 anchovy fillets

1 tablespoon capers

5½ oz (150 g) canned tuna in olive oil

salt and freshly ground black pepper

5½ oz (150 g) lamb's lettuce, to serve

Season the meat with salt and pepper before wrapping it tightly in plastic wrap. Carefully put the meat into a pan of simmering water for approximately 20 minutes, depending on how you like to eat your meat. Once it is cooked, remove the meat from the pan and leave to rest for 1 hour before putting it in the fridge overnight. It will be a lot easier to slice when cold.

To make the sauce mix the egg yolk, mustard and vinegar together in a bowl. While whisking, gradually pour in the oil until the sauce emulsifies. Put all the remaining ingredients in another bowl and, using a hand-held blender, mix together until it is a smooth paste. You may need to add 2 tablespoons of water to get the right consistency. Combine both sauces together and season with salt and pepper.

Usually the veal is sliced very finely, but in this case, cut into rectangles for more texture. Serve with a lot of sauce and well-seasoned lamb's lettuce.

Vietnamese Spring Rolls with Spicy Dipping Sauce

These super-healthy fresh spring rolls summarize just about everything there is to love about Vietnamese food. Once you've mastered the basics, you can play around with this recipe to your heart's content.

Serves 4

2¼ oz (60 g) vermicelli rice noodles

1 tablespoon sesame oil

8 round rice paper wrappers (8 inches / 20 cm)

3½ oz (100 g) cooked pork fillet, finely sliced into 2 inch (4–5 cm) strips

1 carrot, julienned (similar to matchsticks)

1 cucumber, julienned

1 green onion, cut into julienne

1¾ oz (50 g) soybean sprouts

4 tablespoons sweet chili sauce

1 handful of mint leaves

1 handful of cilantro leaves

For the spicy dipping sauce:

1 small red chili, deseeded and finely chopped

1 teaspoon grated ginger

1 teaspoon grated garlic

3 tablespoons fish sauce

1 tablespoon soy sauce

juice of ½ lemon

1 tablespoon finely chopped cilantro

First, make the dipping sauce. Whisk all the ingredients together in a small bowl and leave to infuse for 2 hours. If you are not too keen on "bits," then pass the sauce through a sieve into a small bowl.

Soak the vermicelli in a heatproof bowl of cold water for 20 minutes, then drain and return the noodles to the bowl. Bring a large saucepan of water to a rolling boil and pour over the noodles until they are completely submerged. After 3 minutes they should all become detached and limp. Once tender, drain and lightly rinse under cold water. Once the noodles are at room temperature, place them back into a bowl and mix in the sesame oil to prevent them sticking. Set aside covered with a damp cloth.

Dip the rice paper wrappers, one at a time, in a bowl of warm water, long enough to soften them. Gently remove from the water and lay flat on the work surface or ideally a plastic chopping board. Arrange all the ingredients, except the mint and cilantro leaves, with a dollop of chili sauce together in a line at the top one-third of the paper so there is plenty of surface area left to roll. Begin to roll, carefully and tightly, tucking in the edges as you go along. When halfway, alternately place the mint and cilantro leaves in a line through the middle. These will appear on top of the rolls as a tasty and beautiful decoration.

As you can imagine, eating these fresh as you roll them is best, dipped into the spicy dipping sauce.

Asian-style Stone Bass

Marinating fish is not only super healthy; it's also a great way to pack extra flavor into the delicate flesh. For those who think raw fish can be a little bland, try this recipe out!

Serves 4

2 stone bass fillets, about 1 lb 2 oz (500 g) each

½ garlic clove, very finely chopped

1 small red chilli, deseeded, if desired, and very finely chopped (optional)

1 teaspoon Dijon mustard

1 teaspoon honey

1 tablespoon olive oil

1 teaspoon sesame oil

1 tablespoon soy sauce

1 green onion, chopped

½ bunch of garden cress

finely grated zest of 1 lime

For the marinade:

½ oz (15 g) juniper berries

½ oz (15 g) freshly ground black pepper

9 oz (250 g) fine salt

9 oz (250 g) sea salt

7 oz (200 g) superfine sugar

To serve:

caviar or lump fish eggs (optional)

small salad leaves

various herbs

First, make the marinade in a blender. Blend the juniper berries, pepper and salts, then cover the fish in the salt mixture and sugar and leave to marinate in the fridge for 12 hours. This will season and harden the flesh making it easier to slice.

After 12 hours, rinse the fish and dry with paper towels before using.

Place the garlic and the red chili in a small bowl with the mustard and honey. Drizzle in the oils and the soy sauce and mix together to make an Asian dressing.

Slice the fish into very thin slices and spread it out on a plate, then sprinkle the fish with green onion, salad cress and lime zest. Season with the Asian dressing. To add a bit of glamour you can add a little caviar or lump fish eggs.

This is best served with a fresh salad and mixed herbs.

Green Chicken Curry

Bursting with flavor, there's nothing quite like a homemade curry. Quick and easy to prepare, this recipe will be thoroughly enjoyed by all the family — bold flavors and hugely satisfying.

Serves 4

2 lemongrass sticks

½ inch (1 cm) piece of fresh ginger, peeled

20 oz (600 ml) coconut milk

4 oz (125 ml) chicken stock or water

2 bunches of cilantro (reserve a few leaves for the garnish)

1 lb 2 oz (500 g) chicken thighs, cut into bitesize pieces

2 tablespoons coconut oil

1 white onion, chopped

1 carrot, chopped

1 green chili or small green pepper, halved and seeded

1 teaspoon green curry paste

1 kaffir lime leaf

juice of 1 lemon

1 green onion, finely chopped

salt and freshly ground black pepper

cooked basmati rice, to serve

Blend the lemongrass, ginger, coconut milk, stock and cilantro thoroughly in a powerful blender until the cilantro leaves and lemongrass have completely disappeared. Press the liquid mixture through a sieve, making sure you extract as much liquid as you possibly can. Set aside.

Season the chicken. Heat the coconut oil in a large saucepan over a high heat. Sear the chicken, until beautifully caramelized. Remove from the pan and set aside. (The chicken is purposefully not cooked through as it will continue cooking in the curry later on.)

Add the onion, carrot and green chili to the same pan that the chicken was seared in and mix in the curry paste. Once the vegetables are tender, return the chicken to the pan, then pour over the reserved liquid mixture, add the kaffir lime leaf and bring to a boil. Reduce the heat and simmer for 30 minutes. Season to taste, then add the lemon juice and the green onion. This is best served with basmati rice and the reserved fresh cilantro leaves on top.

Japanese Seaweed Salad with Crayfish Tails

In Japan they eat seaweed for breakfast, lunch and dinner. Sea vegetables have a delicious taste, they are also extremely easy to prepare and are one of the richest sources of minerals around, as well as being virtually fat-free.

Serves 4 as a side

¾ oz (20 g) dehydrated shredded wakame

¼ oz (10 g) dehydrated hijiki

1 tablespoon rice vinegar

2 tablespoons sesame oil

1 tablespoon soy sauce

1 teaspoon yuzu or lime juice

1 teaspoon runny honey

1 teaspoon finely grated ginger

4½ oz (120 g) cooked crayfish tails

½ nori sheet

1 green onion, finely sliced

2 tablespoons toasted white sesame seeds

Place the wakame and hijiki seaweed in a large bowl and pour over enough warm water to cover completely. Soak for 10–20 minutes depending on how firm you like the salad to be.

Meanwhile, in a separate bowl, whisk all the liquids together with the honey and grated ginger to make a Japanese dressing. Once the seaweed is soaked, drain and press between your hands to remove any excess water.

Place the seaweed and crayfish tails in a serving bowl and pour the Japanese dressing on top. Toss all the ingredients together until well combined.

Finely slice the nori sheet into fine spaghetti-like strings using a sharp knife or scissors. Just before serving, sprinkle the finely sliced green onion, sesame seeds and nori all over the salad.

Wakame and hijiki are sea vegetables and can be bought from Asian food stores or purchased online.

Ravioles

Emily: I discovered these amazing gnocchi-like pasta a few years back in a small town in the Occitan Valley in Piedmont. Their unusual name comes from a local dialect of the Occitan language, but these are nothing like traditional Italian ravioli. My husband's "Nonna" would hand-roll them on a wooden surface and serve them with browned butter and Parmesan. This recipe, passed to me by my mother-in-law, isn't for the faint-hearted.

Serves 4

1 lb 9 oz (700 g) potatoes

5½–7 oz (150–200 g) plain flour, plus
    extra for dusting

2¾ oz (75 g) butter

3½ oz (100 g) Parmesan, grated

salt

Cook the potatoes whole in a pan of boiling water until tender. Once cooked, peel and pass through a potato ricer. The potato pulp must still be piping hot when you transfer it to a lightly floured surface. Gradually knead in the flour as you would for a bread dough. You must have the right consistency to be able to roll out the ravioles correctly — not too soft and not too firm.

Roll out the entire potato mix into long sausages of approximately ¾ inch (2 cm) wide. Cut the sausages into small pieces, about ¾ inch (2 cm) long, with a knife. Roll each piece against the floured surface with the palm of your hand to create shape resembling a long, thin gnocchi.

Once all the ravioles have been rolled out, cook them immediately in a pan of boiling salted water for 2 minutes. Drain carefully, as they are very fragile, and place in a warm bowl.

Meanwhile, put the butter in a small saucepan over a medium-low heat and whisk constantly until little browned bits appear on the base. Remove the pan from the heat and pour 2 tablespoons of browned butter over the fresh pasta with some grated Parmesan.

Strawberry Tiramisu

All there is to say is YUM! Joconde biscuit is a light almond sponge cake, named after the Mona Lisa. It is traditionally used in the classic French Opera Cake.

Serves 6–8 and fills a 8½ inch (22 cm) round dessert dish or 6–8 small dessert dishes

8 oz (230 g) fresh strawberries, hulled and cut into small cubes, about ¼ inch (5 mm)

6 oz (175 g) strawberry jam, preferably homemade

1 tablespoon water (optional)

For the strawberry syrup:

3 oz (90 g) superfine sugar

3¼ oz (90 ml) water

2½ oz (70 g) ripe strawberries, chopped

For the Joconde biscuit:

5 whole eggs

4½ oz (125 g) ground almonds

4½ oz (125 g) icing sugar

1 oz (30 g) plain flour

1 oz (30 g) clarified butter, melted and still hot

4 egg whites

1 pinch of salt

For the mascarpone cream:

6 egg yolks

2¾ oz (75 g) superfine sugar

9 oz (250 g) mascarpone

3½ oz (100 ml) whipping cream

1 tablespoon icing sugar

For the caramelized pistachio powder:

4 tablespoons superfine sugar

2 tablespoons water

2¾ oz (75 g) toasted pistachio nuts

To prepare the strawberry syrup, which can be made well in advance, bring the sugar, measured water and strawberries to boil, then reduce the heat and simmer for 4 minutes before removing the pan from the heat. Leave the liquid to cool before passing through a sieve. Set aside.

To prepare the Joconde biscuit, preheat the oven to 350°F (180°C), and line 2 or 3 baking trays with parchment paper. Place the whole eggs, ground almonds and icing sugar in a large bowl. Whisk with a hand-held mixer until foamy and doubled in volume, then gently sift in the flour and add the clarified butter, gently folding everything together with a spatula.

In a separate bowl, whisk the egg whites with a pinch of salt until nice and stiff, then gently stir one-third of the beaten whites to the egg mixture. Finally, pour the entire egg mixture on top of the remaining egg whites and combine gently, making sure not to break the egg whites.

To make the mascarpone cream, make sure that both creams and yolks are cold before you start. Whisk the egg yolks and superfine sugar together in a bowl with a hand-held mixer until white and foamy. Gradually add the mascarpone and beat on a medium speed for at least 8 minutes until the mixture has doubled in volume and has a ribbon texture.

Continues next page...

177

Strawberry Tiramisu **continued**

In a separate bowl, whip the cream and icing sugar together until stiff peaks form and it is smooth and unctuous. Gently fold both mixtures together and store in the fridge until ready to build the tiramisu.

For the caramelized pistachio powder, line a baking tray with parchment paper. Pour the sugar and measured water into a small saucepan over a medium-low heat. Once the sugar has dissolved, increase the heat and boil. No need to stir until the syrup begins to color. At this point add the pistachios and stir with a wooden spoon until it is a beautiful caramel color. Once all the nuts are properly coated, spread them on the prepared baking tray and leave to cool until the caramel has hardened. Once the caramel has hardened, break several bits off and pulse in a powerful blender until ground to a powder. Reserve any leftovers for the decoration.

Mix the strawberries and jam together. If you have quite a liquid jam simply mix both together. If the jam is a little stiff, lightly heat and add the measured water before mixing with the fresh strawberries.

Begin layering a 8½ inch (22 cm) round baking dish. Soak the Joconde biscuit in the strawberry syrup and place a layer on the base of the dish, then evenly spread the jam and strawberry mixture over, followed by the mascarpone cream. Repeat the process until you reach the top of the dish making sure you finish off by sprinkling with the caramelized pistachio powder. Decorate with any leftover caramelized pistachio pieces.

Lychee and Coconut Panna Cotta Infused with Kaffir Lime Leaves

The aromas in this dessert are reminiscent of Asia. Kaffir limes and their leaves deliver unmistakable aromatic flavors and, paired with the delicate sweetness of lychee and coconut, this panna cotta is like no other.

Serves 4–6

For the panna cotta:

14 oz (400 g) can pitted lychees in their liquid

14 oz (400 ml) can coconut milk

1 tablespoon superfine sugar

2 kaffir lime leaves

five $1/16$ in (5 g) sheets of gelatin

1 cup (250 ml) whipping cream

For the crispy coconut flakes:

5½ oz (150 g) coconut flakes

1 pinch of salt

1 tablespoon maple syrup

Preheat the oven to 350°F (180°C).

To prepare the crispy coconut flakes, mix the coconut, salt and maple syrup in a large bowl and stir until the coconut is evenly coated all over. Spread the mixture on a baking sheet and bake in the oven for 20 minutes, stirring every 5–7 minutes, until the coconut flakes are an even golden brown color. Remove from the oven and leave to cool.

For the panna cotta, blend the lychees and their liquid in a powerful food processor until paste-like, then pass through a fine-mesh sieve to form a smooth paste. Place this paste together with the coconut milk, sugar and kaffir lime leaves in a saucepan and bring to a gentle simmer, then remove from the heat. Cover with a lid and leave to infuse for approximately 15 minutes. Remove the kaffir leaves with a slotted spoon and discard.

Soak the gelatin sheets in a bowl of cold water for 2–3 minutes until softened, then squeeze out the excess water and whisk into the warm liquid. Finally, pour in the cream then stir the mixture before using it to fill four to six 7 oz (200 ml) ramekins.

Leave to set in the refrigerator for at least 3 hours. Sprinkle the crispy coconut flakes over the top for that special crunch before devouring.

179

The Professional
Kitchen

Emily

I went to the great Institut Paul Bocuse catering college in France so I have quite a bit of knowledge of traditional French cookery. But since then I have worked both in traditional and more modern restaurants, so the recipes in this chapter are inspired by what I have learned in both. I love to adapt the old techniques and let my imagination take over to create something different. For instance, duck breast is a stalwart of French menus but I have suggested partnering it with asparagus and coffee (see page 200) and my pan-seared pollock is served with avocado and a citrus dressing (see page 184). Both dishes are still very French but with a lighter touch that suits today's tastes — this is the kind of food that I really enjoy.

Some of these recipes, such as the Crispy Rolled Pig's Head with Red Cabbage Salad (see page 219), are quite challenging and take a while to put together, but they are perfectly achievable for the home cook and so worth the effort — mum has tried them in our kitchen. Once in a while it's good to test your skills and try something a little more adventurous.

Pan-seared Pollock with Avocado and Citrus Dressing

Avocado is an incredibly healthy and versatile fruit that can be used in savory dishes. It is grilled in this recipe and puréed with a sharp and tangy citrus dressing. You are sure to impress your guest with this fun dish.

Serves 4

1 lb 12 oz (800 g) pollock fillets, scaled

1 tablespoon olive oil

salt and freshly ground black pepper

coriander cress, to garnish

For the avocado purée:

1½ avocados, peeled and pitted

juice of ½ lemon

2 drops of Tabasco sauce

2 tablespoons olive oil

¼ bunch of cilantro

For the lemon dressing:

4 oz (125 ml) lemon juice

1 tablespoon superfine sugar

3 lemons, peeled and quartered

3 tablespoons olive oil

finely grated zest of ½ lemon

1 pinch of chili powder

½ avocado, peeled and cut into 12 small cubes, about ¼ inch (5 mm)

For the garnish:

2 bok choy, halved

2 tablespoons water

1 tablespoon olive oil

1 avocado, peeled, pitted and cut into segments

To make the lemon dressing, put the lemon juice and sugar with the quartered peeled lemons (do not remove the seeds) into a small saucepan and simmer over a low heat for approximately 40 minutes. Once the lemon chunks have dissolved and the juice has reduced by half, pass through a sieve and set the liquid paste aside to cool. Once the lemon paste has cooled, whisk in a small bowl together with the olive oil. To complete the dressing incorporate the lemon zest, chili powder and avocado cubes before seasoning to taste. Don't discard the leftover avocado half as you will use it in the avocado purée.

To prepare the avocado purée, put the avocados in a powerful blender together with the lemon juice, Tabasco, olive oil, cilantro and a pinch of salt and blend until the purée is silky smooth. You might need to add a little water if the avocados are not ripe enough. Set aside.

Season the fish with salt and pepper before pan-searing skin-side down in the olive oil in a large frying pan over a medium heat. Once the skin is crispy and lightly colored, roughly 3 minutes, turn the fish over and cook for a further 1 minute depending on the size of the fish. Set aside.

For the garnish, sear the bok choy in the same pan for 2 minutes and deglaze with the measured water. Once the water has completely evaporated, the greens should be tender and cooked through.

In a nonstick frying pan drizzle the 1 tablespoon of olive oil, then pan-sear each avocado segment carefully for 2 minutes on each side. Once the avocado segments are colored on each side remove from the pan.

Delicately arrange all the ingredients on 4 plates and garnish with coriander cress.

Spatchcocked Chicken with Morels, Green Onions and Watercress

Deboning is a very classic skill, but not that difficult to master. Nearly any bird can be spatchcocked and cooked the same way. It guarantees crispy skin and easy eating and carving.

Serves 4

1 whole chicken (about 3 lb 3 oz / 1.4 kg)

4 tablespoons olive oil

3 oz (80 g) dried morels or 8½ oz (240 g) fresh morels

1 shallot, finely chopped

1 tablespoon butter

3½ oz (100 ml) *vin jaune* (a sherry-like wine from France's Jura region) or dry sherry

7 oz (200 ml) chicken stock

3½ oz (100 ml) whipping cream

8 green onions, trimmed

3½ oz (100 g) baby watercress

salt and freshly ground black pepper

Place the chicken, breast-side down, on a chopping board and cut through the middle from front to rear with a sharp knife. Carefully follow the bones all the way round until you have removed the whole carcass, cutting through the thigh and wing joint. You should be left with a completely deboned chicken, preferably without any holes in it. Season the chicken flesh with a pinch of salt and pepper.

Heat 2 tablespoons of the olive oil in a large nonstick frying pan over a medium-low heat. When the oil is hot, place the chicken, skin-side down, into the pan. Place a round piece of parchment paper on top of the chicken and put a heavy pan on top to weigh it down and flatten. Leave to cook for 30–40 minutes checking it occasionally. Remove the weight from the chicken and check that the thighs are cooked through and the skin is golden and crisp. Remove from the heat and leave to rest for at least 10 minutes.

Rehydrate the morels in a bowl of warm water for at least 15 minutes. Drain them and check for any remaining grit, rinsing them under cold water if necessary.

Heat 1 tablespoon of the olive oil in a large frying pan over a medium heat. Add the chopped shallot and morels to the pan. Stir until the shallot are translucent, approximately 3 minutes. Season to taste. Add the butter to the pan and let the mushrooms crisp up for a further 3 minutes. Once the morels have absorbed all the fat, deglaze with the *vin jaune*. As soon as the alcohol has evaporated pour the stock into the pan. Leave to simmer and reduce by two-thirds for 5–10 minutes, depending on the pan size. Finally, finish the sauce by incorporating the cream and bringing to a boil for 2 minutes. Check the seasoning again before plating.

Bring a saucepan of salted water to a boil and blanch the green onions for 30 seconds, then refresh in a bowl of iced water. Heat a griddle pan and brush with the remaining olive oil before grilling the green onions, cut-side down, for 4–5 minutes, turning them around occasionally. Once tender and a nice charred color remove them from the heat.

Cut the chicken into 4 pieces and serve with the green onions and peppery watercress.

If you cannot find vin jaune, use a very dry white wine. Vin jaune is not unlike a fino sherry (but unfortified).

Mushroom Agnolotti

The color, texture and flavor of fresh pasta is simply incomparable to dried pasta. It's best to prepare this dish of small, filled pasta squares in spring, when the mushrooms are at their best. Enjoy it as a starter or as a main course with added vegetables.

Serves 4

For the pasta dough:

1 lb 2 oz (500 g) plain flour, plus extra for dusting

1 teaspoon salt

1 teaspoon olive oil, plus extra for drizzling

4 whole eggs

3 tablespoons water (optional)

For the filling:

10½ oz (300 g) white mushrooms or any other wild mushroom, such as porcini or whatever is in season

2¼ oz (60 g) Parmesan, grated

1 handful of walnuts, chopped

1¾ oz (50 g) dried breadcrumbs

½ bunch of chives, chopped

2 tablespoons olive oil

1 garlic clove, finely chopped

1 green onion, finely chopped

3 tablespoons whipping cream

salt and freshly ground black pepper

To make the pasta dough, place the flour, salt, olive oil and beaten eggs in a large bowl and mix together by hand until it is elastic. You may need to add a few tablespoons of water to help knead the dough properly. Wrap the dough in plastic wrap and leave to rest in the fridge overnight.

The next day, to make the filling, chop three-quarters of the mushrooms. Cut the remaining mushrooms into small cubes and set aside in a bowl. Add the grated Parmesan, chopped walnuts, breadcrumbs and chopped chives to the chopped mushrooms and mix together.

Heat the olive oil in a frying pan over a medium heat and fry the garlic and green onion for 2–3 minutes, until tender. Add the chopped mushrooms and season. Once the mushrooms are cooked and have rendered all their water, deglaze the pan with the cream. Transfer the cooked mixture to a blender and blitz until it is a smooth purée, then leave to cool before mixing it in to the other ingredients, including the mushroom cubes. Set the filling aside for at least 2 hours in the fridge before using.

Roll out the pasta dough as finely as you possibly can on a lightly floured surface. It is much easier to use a pasta machine if you have one. The dough will fight you and bounce back but continue until it is 1/16 inch (2 mm) thick. Cut out squares, about 3¼ inches (8 cm) with a sharp knife, then add ½ tablespoon of filling into the center of each square. Brush a little water around the edge of the pasta squares and fold over diagonally. You should get crossed-top agnolotti.

Cook the pasta in a pan of boiling salted water for 4 minutes, then drain and serve, drizzled with some olive oil. You can also add some wild mushrooms or porcini and a meat jus (beef or veal) to accompany the pasta, if you like.

Razor Clams, Mushrooms and Wild Garlic

Many summer holidays were spent trying to trick and catch as many clams as we could for supper.

Serves 1 as a starter

2 raw extra-large razor clams

½ oz (15 g) St George mushrooms

½ oz (15 g) girolles

1 tablespoon olive oil

1 tablespoon butter

½ green onion, finely chopped

1 tablespoon finely sliced wild garlic

1 pinch of *piment d'Espelette* or chili powder

1 pinch of grated lemon zest

1 tablespoon toasted breadcrumbs

salt and freshly ground black pepper

wild garlic flowers, to garnish

Remove the flesh of the clams and discard the stomachs keeping only the muscle. Reserve in a bowl of ice-cold water until ready to use. Clean the clam shells and set aside.

Make sure that all the mushrooms are the same size and dry before cooking them.

Heat the olive oil in a large frying pan over a medium-high heat. When hot, add the mushrooms, season and sauté for 4–8 minutes, or until they have rendered all their water. Add the butter, green onion (only the white part) and the wild garlic.

Meanwhile, diagonally slice the razor clams to make ¾ inch (2 cm) wide lozenges. Add them to the pan and mix in with all the other ingredients. The shellfish will cook extremely quickly, so remove the pan from the heat after 30 seconds. Sprinkle over the *piment d'Espelette* and lemon zest before starting to plate.

Spoon the cooked mixture into both sides of the cleaned razor clam shells and top with toasted breadcrumbs, wild garlic flowers and finely sliced green onion (the green tips).

Octopus Salad with Chili Mayonnaise

Octopus is a great alternative to fish. People tend to shy away when it comes to cooking "the beast," although it is extremely easy. Cooked properly not only is octopus nutritious; it is also amazing in taste and texture.

Serves 4

For the octopus:

1 whole octopus (approx. 4 lb 8 oz / 2 kg) — it will reduce considerably in size once cooked

1 carrot, roughly chopped

1 white onion, roughly chopped

1 bay leaf

4 black peppercorns

1 tablespoon rock salt

butter, for pan roasting

For the mayonnaise:

1 egg yolk

1 teaspoon Dijon mustard

juice of ½ lemon

1 cup (250 ml) neutral oil, such as rapeseed or sunflower

1 pinch each of salt and freshly ground black pepper

1 tablespoon sweet chili sauce

For the salad:

9 oz (250 g) new potatoes, halved

4 tablespoons olive oil

4 oz (125 ml) water

1 pinch each of salt and freshly ground black pepper

3 large green onions, 2 cut in half and thinly sliced

2 green chilies or baby green peppers, seeded

3 heads little gem lettuce (baby romaine), quartered

1 tablespoon butter, plus 1 teaspoon

To prepare the octopus, cut off and discard the head, including the beak, then remove and discard any innards. Place the carrot, onion, bay leaf, peppercorns and rock salt in a large Dutch oven, add approximately 3½ pints (2 liters) water and bring to a boil. Add the octopus and check that the water covers it — add more if it doesn't. Reduce the heat and cook the octopus in simmering water for up to 1½ hours — depending on the size of the octopus — until tender (check frequently with a knife). Once you can easily cut through the flesh, drain the octopus and leave to cool before transferring to the fridge overnight.

The next day, make the mayonnaise. Place the egg yolk in a large bowl. Add the mustard and lemon juice and whisk in the oil, drop by drop, until it is well combined. After a few minutes the sauce will emulsify and thicken. Season to taste with salt and pepper and add the sweet chili sauce.

To make the salad, place the new potatoes in a pan large enough to fit them all in. Add 2 tablespoons of the olive oil and set over a medium heat. Spread out the potatoes flesh-side down and let them color for 5 minutes. Once they have a nice caramelized brown color pour in the measured water and cover the pan with a lid. The steam will cook the potatoes. Once the water has completely evaporated, approximately 8 minutes, season with the salt and pepper and set aside.

Continues next page...

Octopus Salad **continued**

Heat a little olive oil in a frying pan over a medium heat and pan-sear the halved green onions for 2–3 minutes, or until tender, then add the green chilies and pan-sear for 1 minute. Once both the green onions and chilies are tender, remove from the heat and set aside with the potatoes.

Pan-sear the lettuces for a few minutes on each side in 1 teaspoon of butter. The lettuces should not be cooked, just charred to give them extra taste.

Finally, peel any excess skin off the octopus and slice before pan-roasting in 1 tablespoon of butter for 2 minutes on each side. Once the octopus is a beautiful brown, caramelized color, remove from the pan.

Mix all the lukewarm ingredients together with 1 tablespoon of mayonnaise, then divide among serving plates, sprinkled with the finely sliced green onion on top.

Smoked and Roasted Eel with Tea Consommé

The combination of delicately smoked tea and roasted eel takes this dish to a new dimension.

Serves 2

1 red beet, any leaves cut off

1 yellow beet, any leaves cut off

olive oil, for drizzling

4 turnips, trimmed but keep the tops for use in the Radish Top Soup (**see** page 28)

7 oz (200 g) smoked eel

½ tablespoon butter

19 oz (550 ml) clear fish stock

1 tablespoon lapsang souchong tea leaves

1 green onion, finely sliced

salt and freshly ground black pepper

Preheat the oven to 400°F (200°C).

Place the beets on some foil, drizzle with olive oil and season with salt and pepper. Wrap the foil around the beets loosely and place the package on a baking tray. Roast in the oven for 1½ hours (add 30 minutes for larger veggies) until the tip of a knife easily slides through the middle of the beets. Leave the beets to cool until you can handle them, then peel off the skin with paper towels.

Leave baby turnips whole or cut larger turnips into bite-sized pieces. Wrap them loosely in foil with the same seasoning as the beets. Roast the turnips in the oven until tender. Start checking on them after about 30 minutes.

Meanwhile, slice the smoked eel into bite-sized diamond shapes. Heat a drop of olive oil in a nonstick frying pan over a medium-high heat and pan-sear the eel pieces. After 2 minutes, once the eel has a little color, reduce the heat and add the butter to the pan. Roast for a further 2 minutes with the foaming butter, then remove from the pan and set aside on paper towels.

Bring the fish stock to a boil in a medium saucepan. Turn off the heat as soon as the liquid has boiled and sprinkle in the tea leaves. Let the tea infuse for approximately 5 minutes (more or less depending on how strong you enjoy it), then pass through a fine sieve and season with salt and pepper.

Slice all the cooked vegetables into small segments and place in two small serving bowls, then delicately add the roasted eel and sprinkle the green onion on top. Finally, pour over the fish stock.

Duck Breast, Asparagus and Coffee

Duck breast, asparagus and coffee make a fantastic combination in this extraordinary dish. They are served drizzled with a subtle orange-flavored sweet-and-sour sauce based on a classic French gastrique made from caramelized sugar deglazed with vinegar.

Serves 4

2 large duck breasts, with skin

12 green asparagus spears

1 tablespoon olive oil

1 handful of chives, finely sliced

salt and freshly ground black pepper

For the asparagus purée:

1 tablespoon olive oil

12 oz (350 g) white asparagus, peeled and roughly chopped

2 tablespoons butter

1¾ oz (50 ml) whipping cream

1 pinch of finely ground coffee

For the pickled onion:

1 small red onion, sliced into thin rings, about ¹⁄₁₆ inch (1–2 mm) inch thick

¾ oz (20 g) superfine sugar

1 teaspoon salt

½ teaspoon crushed black pepper

1¼ pint (150 ml) white wine vinegar

3½ oz (100 ml) water

1 dried bay leaf

For the gastrique sauce:

2¼ oz (60 g) superfine sugar

4 tablespoons red wine vinegar

juice of 2 oranges

7 oz (200 ml) chicken or vegetable stock

The pickled onion can be prepared well in advance. Place the onion rings in a sterilized preserving jar or bowl. Bring all the other ingredients to a boil in a small saucepan. As soon as it has reached a rolling boil, pour the mixture over the sliced onions. Leave the onion rings to cool before sealing the jar or eating.

To make the asparagus purée, heat the olive oil in a large saucepan over a medium heat and add the chopped asparagus. Stir until the asparagus begin to color, then add the butter to the pan. Leave the butter to foam up for at least 3 minutes before seasoning and covering with a lid. After 5 minutes uncover and check that all the chunks are tender,

then deglaze with the cream and bring to a gentle simmer before pouring everything into a food processor. Blend for 2 minutes until smooth, then pass through a sieve to get rid of any remaining strings. Season the purée to taste with salt, pepper and the ground coffee.

For the gastrique sauce, place the sugar in a dry saucepan and leave to caramelize over a gentle heat. Once the sugar has entirely dissolved, deglaze the pan with the vinegar. Once the liquid has evaporated pour in the orange juice together with the stock and leave to simmer for 5–10 minutes until reduced and thickened.

Score the skin of the duck to allow the fat to render away easily and season with a pinch of salt and pepper. Place a large nonstick frying pan over a medium heat. Once nice and hot, place the breasts, skin-side down, in the pan and dry-fry for approximately 7 minutes until golden brown and crispy. Remove some of the fat from the pan before turning the duck over to cook for a further 4 minutes, depending on the thickness of the meat. Leave to rest for at least 5 minutes before serving.

Snap off the ends of the green asparagus spears and peel the bottom half. Bring a large pot of salted water to a boil and add the asparagus. Cook for 5–8 minutes until tender, then drain and refresh in a bowl of iced water. Heat the olive oil in a frying pan over a medium heat and add the asparagus and cook for 3–10 minutes, until they are a beautiful brown caramelized color. Slice the asparagus into 4 uneven segments and sprinkle the chives all over.

To serve, cut each duck breast lengthways in half, then place a half on each plate. Add a large tablespoon of purée in the center of each plate and place the asparagus spears on top. Drizzle the gastrique sauce around the plate to finish and garnish with pickled onion.

Rabbit *Pâté en Croute*

Don't be put off by the name of this recipe and the complicated techniques it implies. It is easily achievable at home.

Serves 8 as a starter

2 tablespoons butter

1 shallot, sliced

4½ oz (125 g) rabbit or chicken liver

1 thyme sprig

4 tablespoons cognac

4½ oz (125 g) rabbit meat

4½ oz (125 g) unsmoked bacon

2 juniper berries

4½ oz (125 g) terrine of foie gras, cut into small dice

2 lb 4 oz (1 kg) spinach

1 garlic clove, crushed

For the shortcrust pastry:

4¼ oz (120 g) plain flour, plus extra for dusting

1 pinch of fine salt

1 oz (25 g) lard, cubed

1 oz (25 g) butter, cubed

1–2 tablespoons cold water

1 egg yolk mixed with 1 tablespoon milk to use as an egg wash

salt and freshly ground black pepper

To make the pastry, sift the flour and salt into a large mixing bowl. Add the lard together with the butter and rub them between your fingertips until the mixture is crumbly and resembles breadcrumbs. Pour in the water and bring the dough together with your hands, but do not overwork it. Cover the dough and leave to rest in the fridge for 30 minutes before using.

Heat half the butter in a frying pan over a medium heat and cook the shallot for 2–3 minutes, until softened. Increase the heat to high, add the livers and cook until brown and caramelized. Season with salt and pepper, add the thyme and deglaze with the cognac. Once the alcohol has evaporated, leave to cool a little, then transfer to the fridge to cool further.

Preheat the oven to 350°F (180°C).

Mince the rabbit meat, the cooled liver and shallot mixture, the bacon and juniper berries in a mincer, then mix together thoroughly before

seasoning and adding the foie gras. Heat the remaining butter in a frying pan and sauté the spinach and garlic for 3–4 minutes until the spinach is completely wilted, then remove from the heat and leave to cool. Press the cooled spinach in the palms of your hands to extract all the water and form into small round balls.

Line the base and side of a round 6 inch (15 cm) pan with the pastry. Spread the minced meat over the base, followed by a layer of the spinach balls, then repeat the layering process until you reach the top of the pan. Roll out the remaining pastry into a thin round to the diameter of your tin to create a lid and brush all over with the egg wash. Cook in the oven for 30–40 minutes.

Variation: For a professional finish you can reduce 1 cup (250 ml) chicken stock and add to the pâté by making a small hole in the center of the lid. Pour the stock inside only once the pâté is cooked and has been chilled overnight. Thanks to this you will achieve a beautiful meaty jelly.

Pan-seared Mackerel with Cucumber Tagliatelle

Mackerel is the cheapest fish on the market and is invariably oozing with taste.

Serves 4

6 mackerel fillets, about 10–10½ oz (280–300 g) each

1 cucumber, peeled and cut in half lengthways

2 oz (50 ml) water

3½ oz (100 ml) white wine vinegar

1¾ oz (50 g) superfine sugar

2 tablespoons olive oil

3½ oz (100 g) Greek yogurt

1 pinch of paprika

2 mint leaves, finely chopped

1 green onion, very finely sliced

finely grated zest of 1 lime

salt and freshly ground black pepper

For the marinade:

¾ oz (20 g) salt per 2 lb 4 oz (1 kg) mackerel

¹⁄₁₀ oz (2 g) sugar per 2 lb 4 oz (1 kg) mackerel

Place the mackerel in a shallow dish and sprinkle the salt and sugar over the top. Allow to marinate for 45 minutes before cooking as this will help tenderize and begin to cook the flesh. Carefully wash the marinade off and pat dry with paper towels before cooking.

With one half of the cucumber make long tagliatelle-like strips with the help of a mandolin or a vegetable peeler, then bring the measured water, vinegar and sugar to a boil in a pan and add the cucumber strips. Remove the pan from the heat and leave to cool. Once cooled, you should have some tangy cucumber "tagliatelle." Discard the remaining liquid.

Cut the other half of the cucumber into chunks and sear them in a frying pan with 1 tablespoon of the olive oil until golden brown. In the same heated pan, sear the mackerel with the remaining oil until the skin is nice and crispy. Set the mackerel aside until they are cold before cutting them into bite-sized pieces. Season the yogurt with salt, pepper, paprika and finely chopped mint. Plate everything together and scatter the green onion and lime zest over the top.

Crispy Sweetbreads, Asparagus and Almond Purée

The whole Roux clan love sweetbreads. The tender and moist texture combined with the crispy exterior is simply heavenly.

Serves 4

1 lb 12 oz (800 g) raw veal sweetbreads

1 bunch of cherry tomatoes

12 thin green asparagus

2 tablespoons olive oil, plus a drizzle for baking

a handful of plain flour, for dusting

salt and freshly ground black pepper

For the almond purée:

3½ oz (100 g) blanched almonds

7 oz (200 ml) milk

3½ oz (100 ml) whipping cream

For the jus:

2 cups (500 ml) veal stock

7 oz (200 ml) tomato juice

1 oz (30 g) pitted black olives, halved

It is best to soak the sweetbreads for several hours in clean cold water to remove any impurities.

Preheat the oven to 350°F (180°C).

Bring a large pot filled with salted water to a gentle simmer before adding the raw sweetbreads. Depending on the size, cook them for 15–20 minutes making sure the water never boils. Delicately remove the offal from the water and immediately refresh in a bowl of ice-cold water. Trim off any sinew or gristle and pat dry with paper towels. Set aside.

To create a simple and light jus to accompany the dish, reduce the stock and tomato juice in 2 separate saucepans for 5–10 minutes until they are both reduced by two-thirds. Pour one into the other and whisk them together, then add the halved olives and season to taste. Set aside.

To make the almond purée, place the blanched almonds in a medium saucepan with the milk and cream and bring to a gentle simmer. Cook for 10 minutes, then while still hot, transfer the almonds and liquid directly to a food processor and blend until completely smooth. Season well.

Place the cherry tomatoes and asparagus spears in a large bowl and carefully season the veggies with a drizzle of olive oil, salt and pepper. Place on a baking tray and cook in the oven for 12–15 minutes, until the asparagus are tender and the tomatoes are shriveled up.

Meanwhile, season each sweetbread with salt and pepper and lightly dust in flour. Heat the 2 tablespoons of olive oil in a frying pan over a medium-high heat and pan-fry the sweetbreads for approximately 3–5 minutes on each side. Avoid moving them too often in the pan, in order to achieve that beautiful crispy brown color.

Elegantly dress all the different elements together and devour.

Confit Pork, Kale and Kabocha Purée

This is a colorful and healthy recipe that always pleases a crowd. Kale is an extremely popular vegetable, known for its numerous health benefits. It is also full of flavor and simply very pretty to look at.

Serves 4

1 lb 9 oz (700 g) pork belly

2 tablespoons olive oil

salt and freshly ground black pepper

For the pumpkin purée:

1 whole kabocha squash (approx. 1 lb 4 oz / 550 g)

1 oz (30 ml) olive oil, plus 1 tablespoon for cooking

1 tablespoon Dijon mustard

For the garnish:

3½ oz (100 g) sprouting broccoli

3½ oz (100 g) flower sprouts (cross between a sprout and a baby cabbage) or Tuscan kale

3½ oz (100 g) purple kale

2 tablespoons olive oil

1 garlic clove, crushed

For the glaze:

7 oz (200 ml) pork or chicken stock

1 teaspoon butter

Place the pork belly in a vacuum bag with a pinch of salt and pepper. Seal firmly in a vacuum pack machine and cook in a water bath at 190°F (90°C) for 3½ hours.

Remove the meat from the water bath and place the bag in iced water to immediately stop cooking. Leave the pork belly to cool in the fridge for a further 45 minutes in order to harden and make it easier to slice. Portion the pork belly into slices of approximately 1½–2 inches (4–5 cm) wide.

Meanwhile, rinse the squash under cold water to get rid of any residual dirt. Cut it in half and remove the seeds with a spoon. If the skin is thin enough, don't bother peeling it as it will give extra taste and texture to the purée. Roughly chop the squash into bite-sized chunks before searing in a shallow saucepan with 1 tablespoon olive oil. After 2 minutes the chunks should be lightly colored. Cover the saucepan with a lid and reduce the heat (by doing so, the kabocha will render water) and cook for approximately 20

minutes until tender throughout and all the water has evaporated from the pan. While still hot, transfer the pumpkin to a powerful blender together with the Dijon mustard, then add the 1 oz (30 ml) olive oil, drop by drop, until the purée emulsifies and thickens. Season to taste with salt and pepper and set aside.

To make the glaze, place the stock in a small saucepan over a low heat and leave to simmer and reduce until the stock becomes a darker color, nearly syrup-like, about 5–10 minutes. Once you have the right texture, remove from the heat and whisk in the butter. Set aside.

Blanch the sprouting broccoli and flower sprouts together in a pan of heavily salted boiling water for 2 minutes. This will help to keep the beautiful color of the vegetables and precook them. Drain carefully and place in a bowl of ice-cold water. Repeat the same process with the purple kale. Heat the olive oil in a large pan over a medium-high heat. Add the crushed garlic together with

the flower sprouts, broccoli and kale. Move the greens around with tongs, so as not to burn them and sprinkle with salt and pepper. Cook and crisp up for 1 minute.

Pan-sear each portion of pork belly in a large frying pan with a drizzle of olive oil over a medium-high heat. Once all the pieces are

a lovely brown caramelized color reduce the heat and add the reserved sauce to the pan. Spoon the sauce over each portion of pork to glaze it until it is completely covered in sauce. Serve with the pumpkin purée and pan-fried vegetables.

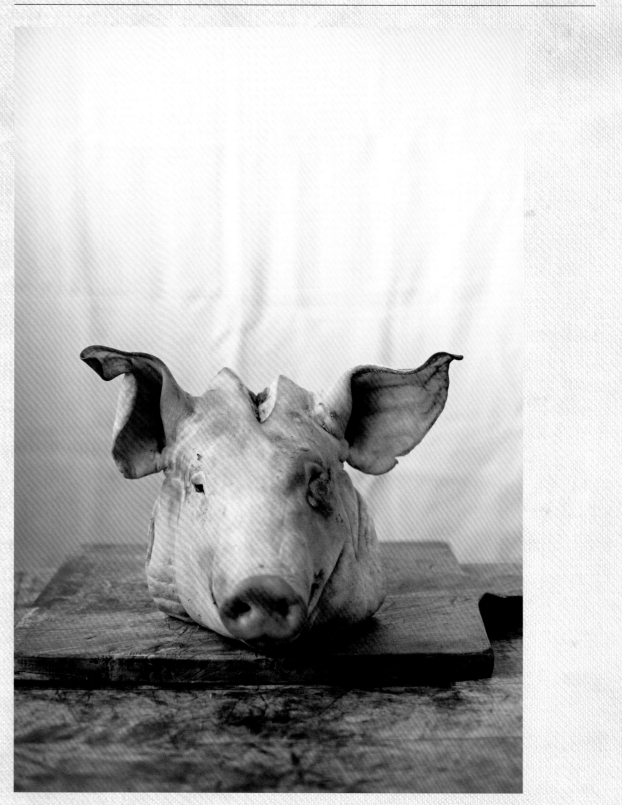

Crispy Rolled Pig's Head with Red Cabbage Salad

Although this recipe is not for the squeamish, it is absolutely delectable and you can prepare it well in advance.
This is a truly wholesome dish that will surprise your guests for sure.

Serves 4

1 pig's head

12 oz (350 g) red cabbage, finely
    shredded

2 tablespoons hazelnut oil

2 tablespoons flaked hazelnuts

1 handful of parsley leaves

finely grated zest of ½ a lemon

1 teaspoon honey

1 tablespoon lemon juice

1 tablespoon olive oil

1 generous pinch of Quatre Épices
    spice blend, to season

salt and freshly ground black pepper

For the bouillon:

1 carrot, roughly chopped

1 white onion, roughly chopped

1 celery stick, roughly chopped

1 star anise

1 bay leaf

1 cinnamon stick

4 black peppercorns

Preheat the oven to 350°F (180°C).

Usually your butcher would have removed all excess hair on the pig's head; however, if any is left, use a kitchen blowtorch to remove them. Using a sharp knife, cut all the way down the middle of the head to the snout and follow the bone structure with your knife. Cut the skin and muscle away from the bone until you end up with 2 rectangular pieces of meat with no holes in them.

Season the meat with a pinch of salt, pepper and the four spices before rolling the pig's head tightly, making sure the ears and snout are folded inside. Tie kitchen string all the way around the rolled head to keep everything in place (as you would with a roast). Place the head in a large casserole dish with the bouillon ingredients and cover with water. Cook in simmering water for about 4 hours. If necessary, top up with water during cooking as the head must always be submerged.

Once tender, cooked through and you can easily pierce the meat with a skewer, remove the head, leave to cool, then wrap in plastic wrap to keep its shape. Leave in the fridge overnight.

The next day, cover the shredded cabbage with ice-cold water and leave to stand for 15 minutes. Drain. Meanwhile, heat the hazelnut oil in a wok or large frying pan over a high heat. Once the wok is piping hot, sprinkle in the cabbage and toss around for 2 minutes. You must keep the crunch and freshness of the raw vegetable. Remove from the heat, place in a bowl and incorporate the remaining ingredients, except the olive oil.

At the last minute, cut the pig's head into thick slices and pan-sear with the olive oil in a frying pan over a medium heat for 4–5 minutes on each side until caramelized and beautifully crispy. Serve with the red cabbage salad.

219

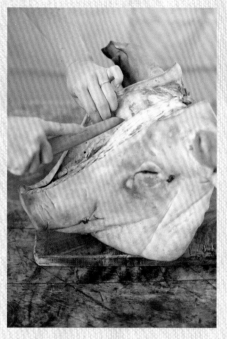

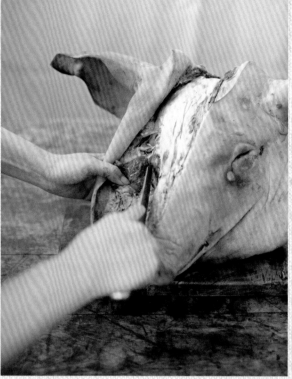

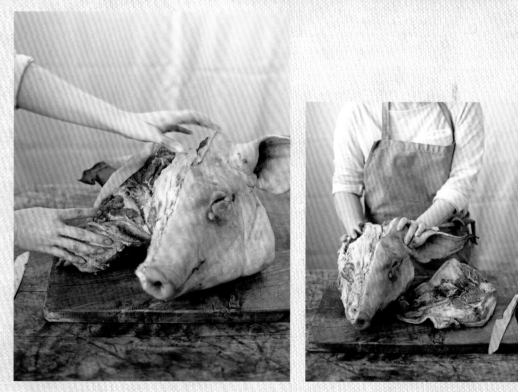

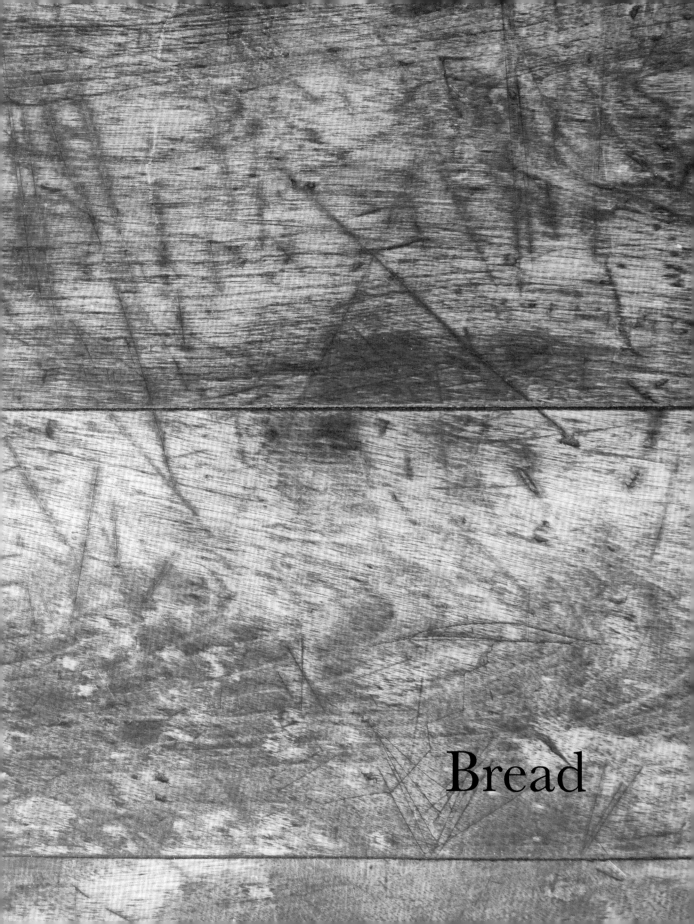

Bread

Giselle

I don't agree with the idea that bread is bad for you. Good bread — not the plastic stuff — is a healthy, nourishing food and our family loves it.

When I was growing up my mother made all our bread. We ate lots of it as children, and I still eat it several times a day. When I first came to the UK in the late 1970s, I found that there wasn't much "proper" bread available — just sliced white loaves in plastic bags. There were bakers but they all seemed to make the same loaf and there was certainly nothing that tasted like the bread I had grown up with. Things have changed, but back then the only thing for me to do was to make my own bread and I still do — three times a week. A lot of the recipes on the following pages are family favorites — things my mother used to make, including Baguettes (see page 236) and *Pain au Lait* (see page 243). Others are my own twists on classic breads, such as *fougasse* (see page 240) and rye bread (see page 232), that I have developed over the years.

When I bake bread I don't measure anything — I do it by eye and feel — so when writing the recipes for this book I had to measure everything very carefully, which I found quite tricky! Be prepared to adapt recipes when baking, as bread can vary according to the weather or the humidity on the day. Sometimes you may need less flour, or the dough may take longer to rise some days than on others. That's the magic of making bread.

Mother Dough

It is so easy to make your own mother dough and keep it going for however long you like. Our own mother dough is nearly 5 years old and you can really tell the difference in flavor.

Makes 1 starter or Mother Dough

1 small bottle of beer
unbleached wheat flour
lukewarm water

Open the bottle of beer and leave it to settle for 5–6 days, until all the bubbles have dispersed and it is completely flat. Pour 1¼ cup (¼ pint) of beer into a small mixing bowl and add 3 tablespoons of flour. Stir to combine (the mixture should achieve a creamy consistency), cover with

something porous (such as muslin or a kitchen towel), then set aside in a warm place.

After approximately 3 days the mixture will begin to bubble and start to smell like yeast. At this stage, add another 4 tablespoons flour and 1¼ cup (¼ pint) water. Stir to combine, then set aside in a warm place. From day 3 onwards, feed the dough with 2 tablespoons flour and 2 tablespoons water every other day.

On days 4 and 5, not much will appear to be happening and the mixture will look fairly lifeless. Don't be concerned — the bacteria contained in the mixture is beginning to die back, making way for the yeast to spring into action.

On day 6, 7 or 8 the mixture will suddenly come to life, doubling in volume after each feeding and releasing a yeasty aroma and lots of bubbles. This indicates that yeast is present and you now have a starter. At this stage you can store the starter in the fridge, but don't forget to feed it with an amount of flour and water equivalent to that removed every time you use some (so, for example, if you remove 4½ oz /120 g of the Mother Dough, feed it with 2¼ oz / 60 ml water and 2¼ oz / 60 g flour).

Everyday Loaves

This basic bread recipe is very versatile and can easily be adapted to include any nuts or dried fruit that you have to hand, making the end result even more special. Walnuts, pumpkin seeds, raisins or dried cranberries, or a combination of all of these, work especially well. Khorasan flour, also known as kamut flour, is a nutritious wholegrain flour with a slightly nutty flavor.

makes 2 — 2 lb (900 g) loaves

butter, for greasing

3¼ oz (90 g) Mother Dough (**see** page 228)

3½ oz (100 g) white spelt flour

14 oz (400 g) Khorasan flour

14 oz (400 ml) water

1 teaspoon fine sea salt

1 tablespoon honey

1 tablespoon Greek yogurt

Lightly grease two 2 lb (900 g) loaf pans with butter.

Place all of the ingredients in a large bowl or the bowl of a stand mixer. Using your hands or the mixer, bring everything together to form a sticky dough. Continue to work the dough for 5 minutes, until smooth, then divide the mixture between the 2 loaf tins. Cover with cling film and set aside to rise at room temperature for up to a day, or until bubbles start to form in the dough. The time it takes to rise will vary depending on the weather, so check your dough every couple of hours to gauge its progress.

Twenty minutes before you want to bake your bread, preheat the oven to 475°F (240°C), and place a roasting pan in the base of the oven.

Once the loaves have risen, remove the plastic wrap and place the tins in the middle of the oven, adding a couple of glasses of cold water to the roasting pan at the base of the oven to create steam and help your bread rise. Bake for 15 minutes, then turn the oven down to 400°F (200°C), and continue to bake for another 40 minutes, until the loaves sound hollow when tapped on their bases.

Leave the loaves to cool slightly in their tins before turning out and cooling to room temperature. The loaves are best eaten on the day of making.

Irish Soda Bread

This recipe is a joy because the dough doesn't need to rise, meaning that you can have fresh bread on the table within an hour of starting.

makes 2 — 2 lb (900 g) loaves

butter, for greasing

13 oz (375 g) whole-wheat flour

8 oz (225 g) self-raising flour

3½ oz (100 g) wheat bran

1¾ oz (50 g) jumbo porridge oats

2½ oz (70 g) steel-cut oats

½ oz (15 g) sea salt

2 teaspoons superfine sugar

1 oz (25 g) baking soda

2 lb 4 oz (1 kg) buttermilk

¾ oz (20 g) molasses

Preheat the oven to 400°F (200°C), and lightly grease two 2 lb (900 g) loaf tins with butter.

Place all of the dry ingredients into the bowl of a stand mixer and whisk together to combine. Pour in the buttermilk and treacle and whisk on a low speed for 5 minutes, then turn the speed up to high and whisk for a further 2 minutes.

Divide the dough between the prepared loaf tins and transfer to the middle of the oven to bake for 50 minutes, until the loaves sound hollow when tapped on their bases. Turn the bread out of the tins and leave to cool on a wire rack before slicing.

Rye Bread with Walnuts and Raisins

This loaf doesn't need a lot of kneading, so can easily be made by hand. Rye flour produces a denser, darker and richer bread that is perfect for the colder seasons and makes a delicious accompaniment to warming winter soups.

makes 2 — 2 lb (900 g) loaves

2 tablespoons olive oil, plus extra for greasing

8¼ oz (230 g) rye flour

12 oz (350 g) strong white bread flour

4¼ oz (120 g) Mother Dough (**see** page 228)

14½ oz (415 g) lukewarm water

2¾ oz (75 g) raisins

3½ oz (100 g) walnut halves

¼ oz (10 g) fine sea salt

1 teaspoon honey

Lightly grease two 2 lb (900 g) loaf tins with olive oil.

Place all of the ingredients in a large bowl and, using your hands, bring everything together to form a sticky dough. Continue to work the dough for 5 minutes, until smooth, then divide the mixture between the 2 tins. Cover with plastic wrap and set aside to rise at room temperature for up to a day, or until bubbles start to form in the dough. The time it takes to rise will vary depending on the weather, so check your dough every couple of hours to gauge its progress.

Twenty minutes before you want to bake your bread, preheat the oven to 475°F (240°C), and place a roasting pan in the base of the oven.

Once the loaves have risen, remove the plastic wrap and place the tins in the middle of the oven, adding a couple of glasses of cold water to the roasting pan at the base of the oven to create steam and help your bread rise. Bake for 15 minutes, then turn the oven down to 400°F (200°C), and continue to bake for another 40 minutes, until the loaves sound hollow when tapped on their bases.

Leave the loaves to cool slightly in their tins before turning out and cooling to room temperature. The loaves are best eaten on the day of making.

Buckwheat Bread

Traditionally used to make blinis, the flavorsome flour in this bread has a distinct taste and color. We have added a sprinkle of chia seeds on top for added "nuttiness."

makes 2 — 2 lb (900 g) loaves

olive oil, for greasing

4¼ oz (120 g) Mother Dough (**see** page 228)

8¼ oz (230 g) buckwheat flour

10½ oz (300 g) strong white flour

15 oz (430 g) lukewarm water

¼ oz (10 g) sea salt

1 tablespoon honey

1 tablespoon Greek yogurt

chia seeds, for sprinkling

Lightly grease two 2 lb (900 g) loaf tins with olive oil.

Place all of the ingredients in a large bowl and, using your hands, bring everything together to form a sticky dough. Continue to work the dough energetically for 5 minutes, until smooth (we tend to do this by hand but an electrical mixer could make the process a lot easier), then divide the mixture between the 2 tins. Cover with cling film and set aside to rise at room temperature for up to a day, or until bubbles start to form in the dough. The time it takes to rise will vary depending on the weather, so check your dough every couple of hours to gauge its progress.

Twenty minutes before you want to bake your bread, preheat the oven to 475°F (240°C), and place a roasting pan in the base of the oven. Once the loaves have risen, remove the plastic wrap, sprinkle with chia seeds, and place the tins in the middle of the oven, adding a couple of glasses of cold water to the roasting pan at the base of the oven to create steam and help your bread rise. Bake for 20 minutes, then turn the oven down to 410°F (210°C), and continue to bake for another 20 minutes. Finally, take the loaves out of the oven, carefully remove them from their tins, then return them to the oven and bake for a further 5 minutes, until the loaves sound hollow when tapped on their bases.

Leave the loaves to cool to room temperature on a wire rack. Eat on the day of making or place in sealable plastic bags and keep in the fridge for several days.

Baguettes

Of all the French breads, the baguette is the most iconic and, with its perfect combination of deliciously crunchy crust and beautifully soft interior, it's not hard to see why.

makes 4 baguettes

¼ oz (10 g) fresh yeast

13 oz (375 g) lukewarm water

1 lb 2 oz (500 g) strong white flour, plus extra for flouring

½ oz (12 g) fine sea salt

olive oil, for greasing

Place the yeast in a small bowl with 2 tablespoons of the lukewarm water and stir until the yeast is completely dissolved.

Sift the flour into the bowl of a stand mixer fitted with a dough hook. Add the salt to the bowl and mix to distribute throughout the flour. Make a well in the center of the flour and add three-quarters of the remaining water, followed by the dissolved yeast. With the mixer on a medium speed, leave to mix for 7 minutes, gradually adding the remaining water as the dough comes together. Once your dough is smooth and elastic transfer it to a lightly oiled bowl, cover with a clean kitchen towel, and set aside to rise at room temperature for 1½ hours, or until doubled in size. Meanwhile, line 2 large baking sheets with parchment paper.

Once the dough has risen, turn it out onto a lightly floured surface and knock back to remove any air bubbles. Divide the dough into 4 even-sized pieces and form each piece into a 12–14 inch (30–35 cm) oblong. Place the baguettes on the prepared baking sheets and set aside to prove at room temperature for 1½ hours.

Preheat the oven to 450°F (230°C).

Once the baguettes have proved, make several diagonal slashes on the top of each with a serrated knife and gently brush the tops with a little cold water. Transfer to the oven to bake for 25 minutes, until golden brown and crisp. Transfer to a wire rack to cool before slicing. These are best eaten the same day they are made.

Pan-bagnat with Sun-dried Tomatoes and Olives

Pan-bagnat *is a sandwich and street food speciality in Nice and Provence. The rolls are traditionally filled with the components of a classic Niçoise salad and eaten on the go, making them the perfect addition to any picnic.*

makes 2 loaves

1 lb 5 oz (600 g) strong white flour, plus extra for dusting

¼ oz (10 g) fresh yeast

1 tablespoon olive oil, plus extra for greasing

14 oz (400 ml) lukewarm water

2 teaspoons fine sea salt

2¾ oz (75 g) pitted green or black olives, roughly chopped

1½ oz (40 g) sundried tomatoes, roughly chopped

Sift the flour into a large bowl and add the yeast, crumbling it with your hands and rubbing it into the flour until you achieve a texture like fine breadcrumbs. Make a well in the center of the flour mixture and pour in the olive oil and water. Using your hands, gradually bring the dry ingredients into the wet, then vigorously knead to form a sticky dough. Add the salt, olives and sundried tomatoes and mix again to distribute throughout the dough.

Turn the dough out onto a lightly floured work surface and knead vigorously for 5 minutes, until it is smooth and no longer sticky. Transfer the dough to a lightly oiled bowl, cover with a clean kitchen towel, and set aside to rise at room temperature for 1½ hours, or until doubled in size. Meanwhile, line 2 large baking sheets with parchment paper. Once the dough has risen, turn it out onto a lightly floured work surface and

knock back to remove any air bubbles. Divide the dough into 2 equal-sized pieces and shape each into a large, tight ball. Place the loaves on the prepared baking sheets and set aside to prove at room temperature, uncovered, for 1 hour.

Preheat the oven to 475°F (240°C), and place a roasting pan in the base of the oven.

Once the dough has proved, transfer to the middle of the oven, adding a couple of glasses of cold water to the roasting pan at the base of the oven to create steam and help your bread rise. Bake for 10 minutes, then reduce the oven temperature to 375°F (190°C), and bake for another 30 minutes, until golden brown and crisp. Transfer to a wire rack to cool before eating.

Rosemary and Black Olive *Fougasse*

This traditional and attractive southern French bread is usually made with crisped lardons or good quality black olives. This is delicious eaten as it is, but spread with tapenade and anchoïade it makes a perfect pre-dinner snack.

Makes 1 *fougasse*

5½ oz (150 g) strong white flour, plus extra for dusting

3½ oz (100 g) self-raising flour

⅛ oz (6 g) fresh yeast

2 tablespoons olive oil, plus extra for greasing

5 oz (150 ml) lukewarm water

1 teaspoon fine sea salt

1½ oz (40 g) pitted black olives, roughly chopped

½ rosemary sprig, leaves chopped

Sift both flours into a large bowl and add the yeast, crumbling it with your hands and rubbing into the flour until you achieve a texture like fine breadcrumbs. Make a well in the center of the flour mixture and pour in the olive oil and water. Using your hands, gradually bring the dry ingredients into the wet, then vigorously knead to form a sticky dough. Add the salt, olives and rosemary to the dough and mix again to distribute throughout the dough.

Turn the dough out onto a lightly floured work surface and knead vigorously for 5 minutes, or until it is smooth and no longer sticky. Transfer the dough to a lightly oiled bowl and set aside to rise at room temperature, covered with a clean kitchen towel, for 1½ hours, or until doubled in size. Meanwhile, line a 12 × 8 inch (30 × 20 cm) baking sheet with parchment paper.

Once the dough has risen, turn it out onto a lightly floured work surface and knock back to remove any air bubbles. Roll or press your dough out to form a large rectangle, roughly the size of your prepared baking sheet. Transfer the dough to your baking sheet and press the dough again to fill right up to the edges. Using a sharp knife, make a long vertical incision down the center of the *fougasse*, leaving the dough intact at the top and bottom. Now make 3 diagonal slashes on either side of the central slash. Once finished the bread should resemble a leaf. Lightly brush the *fougasse* with olive oil and set aside to prove at room temperature, uncovered, for 1 hour.

Preheat the oven to 450°F (230°C), and place a roasting pan in the base of the oven.

Once the dough has proved, place it in the middle of the oven, adding a couple of glasses of cold water to the roasting pan at the base of the oven to create steam and help your bread rise. Bake for 8 minutes, then reduce the oven temperature to 400°F (200°C), and bake for another 10 minutes, until golden brown and crisp. This is best eaten the same day it is made.

Pizza Dough

Whatever toppings you and your family prefer, the key to a good pizza is a thin and crispy base. This recipe makes enough for four large pizzas, but you can portion and freeze your dough before proving for use at a later date.

makes 4 — 12 inch (30 cm) pizza bases

2 lb 4 oz (1 kg) plain flour

1 oz (30 g) fresh yeast

3½ oz (100 g) olive oil, plus extra for greasing

1 lb 5 oz (600 g) lukewarm water

¾ oz (20 g) fine sea salt

Place the flour, yeast, olive oil and 14 oz (400 ml) of the water in the bowl of a stand mixer fitted with a dough hook. Beat on a medium speed for at least 2 minutes until the dough begins to form a ball.

Dissolve the salt in the remaining water and pour gradually into the dough until it is all incorporated, then leave to mix for 5–10 minutes, until the dough has formed a smooth ball. Transfer the dough to a lightly oiled bowl and cover with a damp kitchen towel. Set aside to rise at room temperature for 2 hours, or until the dough has doubled in size.

Once the dough has risen, turn it out onto a lightly floured bowl or surface and divide it into 4 equal-sized pieces. Roll each piece out to form a 12 inch (30 cm) round, about ¼ inch (5 mm) thick. Transfer to a floured pizza or baking tray and set aside to prove at room temperature for 30 minutes.

Preheat the oven to 425°F (220°C).

Once the dough has proved, add your toppings and transfer to the oven to bake for 10 minutes, then reduce the oven temperature to 400°F (200°C), and cook for another 10 minutes. Serve the pizzas hot.

Pain au Lait

These small brioche-like rolls are perfect for weekend mornings when you have a little time to sit and relax over breakfast. They are deliciously soft and light and make the ideal accompaniment to homemade jams and preserves.

makes 25 small rolls

1 lb 1 oz (480 g) plain flour, plus extra for flouring

½ oz (15 g) granulated sugar

1 teaspoon fine sea salt

1¾ oz (50 g) butter, cubed

11¾ oz (340 ml) whole milk

½ oz (15 g) fresh yeast

2 egg yolks, beaten

Sift the flour into a large bowl, then add the sugar and salt and mix to combine. Add the cubed butter to the bowl and, using your hands, rub the butter into the flour until the mixture looks like fine breadcrumbs. Set aside.

Place the milk and yeast in a small pan over a low heat. Mix until the yeast has dissolved into the milk and the liquid is warm, but not hot.

Make a well in the center of the dry ingredients and pour in the milk, then use your hands to bring everything together to a sticky dough. Turn the dough out onto a lightly floured work surface and knead for around 5 minutes, until smooth and elastic. Transfer the dough to a lightly floured bowl and set aside to rise at room temperature, covered, for 1 hour, or until doubled in size. Meanwhile, line 2 large baking trays with parchment paper.

Once the dough has risen, turn it out onto a lightly floured work surface and knock back to remove any air bubbles. Divide the dough into 25 equal-sized pieces and roll into tight balls in the cupped palms of your hands. Transfer the shaped dough to the prepared baking trays, leaving enough space between each to allow them to expand. Set aside to prove at room temperature for 1 hour, or until almost doubled in size.

Preheat the oven to 400°F (200°C).

Brush the tops of the rolls with the egg yolk and transfer to the oven to bake for 10–15 minutes, until golden and well risen. Transfer to a wire rack to cool.

243

Chocolate-filled Brioche

The dough for these brioche is prepared the night before baking and then left to proof slowly in the fridge overnight, meaning that they can be on the table quickly the next morning for an indulgent and impressive weekend breakfast.

Makes 10 small brioche

9 oz (250 g) plain flour

¼ oz (7 g) fresh yeast

3½ oz (100 ml) whole milk

4 tablespoons granulated sugar

seeds from 1 vanilla pod

2 egg yolks

1 teaspoon fine sea salt

4½ oz (125 g) butter, cubed, at room temperature, plus extra for greasing

4½ oz (125 g) dark chocolate (at least 70 percent cocoa solids), broken into cubes

1 egg, beaten

The evening before you bake the brioche, sift the flour into the bowl of a stand mixer fitted with a dough hook. Add the yeast and mix at a slow speed for 2 minutes to combine.

Place the milk, sugar and vanilla seeds in a small pan over a medium heat. Heat until the sugar has dissolved and the milk has just warmed. Take off the heat and whisk the egg yolks into the pan.

Make a well in the center of the flour and yeast mixture and pour in the milk and egg mixture, followed by the salt. With the mixer at a medium speed, mix for around 5 minutes, until the dough has formed into a smooth ball. With the mixer still running, add the butter a cube at a time until it is all incorporated into the dough. Transfer the dough to a lightly floured bowl, cover with plastic wrap and transfer to the fridge to rise overnight.

The next morning, preheat the oven to 400°F (200°C), and grease a muffin pan with butter.

Remove the risen dough from the fridge and divide into 10 equal-sized pieces. On a floured surface, press each of the dough pieces out flat and place a cube of the chocolate in the center. Bring the edges of the dough up to enclose the chocolate and pinch together to seal. Using the cupped palm of your hand, form the chocolate-filled dough pieces into ball shapes and transfer to the prepared muffin pan. Brush the tops of the brioches with beaten egg and transfer to the oven to bake for 15–20 minutes, until golden and well risen.

Immediately turn the brioches out of the pan and leave to cool slightly on a wire rack. Serve warm, with the chocolate melted and oozy in the center.

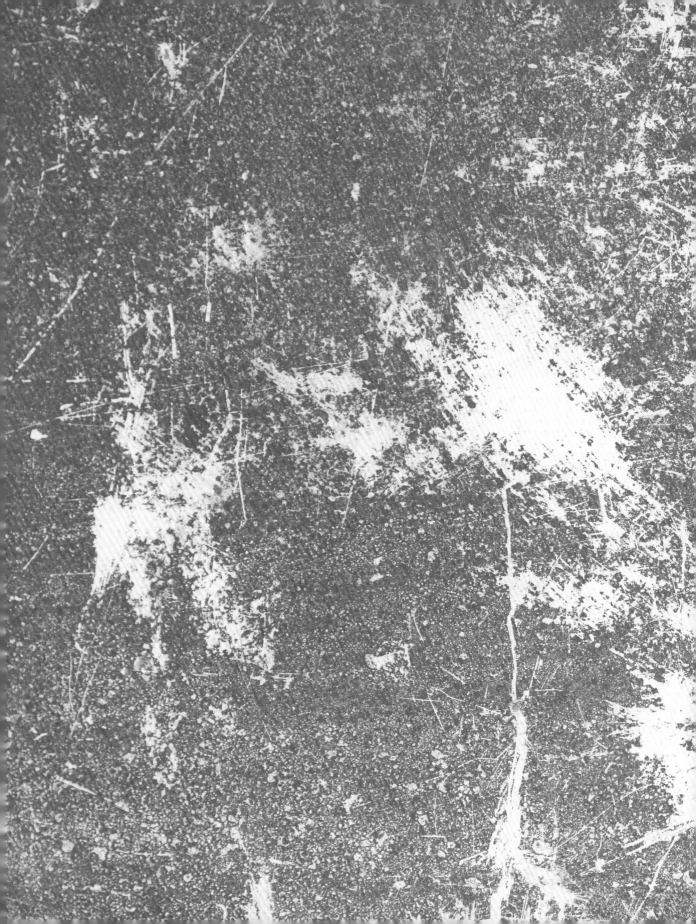

Preserves, Pickles
and Terrines

Giselle

As my family grew most of our food, there were times of the year when we inevitably had gluts of certain ingredients. We'd have more peas, beans, tomatoes or apricots than we could eat. Nothing could be wasted and we had no freezer in those days, so my mother would preserve whatever she could. Her storeroom was lined with jar upon jar of preserved vegetables to use throughout the winter months. She would bottle lovely ripe fruit, make jam and cook up huge batches of tasty tomato and basil sauce that we would enjoy all year round. We would all help, of course. When peas were in season, for instance, my father would unload mountains of them onto the kitchen table for us to pod. The first one to fill their bowl would be let off chores that night, making it a fiercely contested competition.

I love preserving and still more or less follow my mother's methods.

Sterilize each pickle or preserve jar and lid by washing them thoroughly in hot, soapy water, running them through a dishwasher or placing them in a large pan of simmering water for 5–10 minutes. Remove with tongs and leave to drain and dry before filling and water-bath canning, if required (**see** page 251).

Sweet Preserves

Here are a few guidelines to follow when making sweet preserves at home.

For Fruit in Syrup:

Light fruit (e.g. plums):

4 cups (1 liter) water to 9 oz (250 g) sugar

Medium-weight fruit (e.g. peaches):

4 cups (1 liter) water to 12 oz (350 g) sugar

Heavy fruit (e.g. pineapple):

4 cups (1 liter) water to 1 lb 7 oz (650 g) sugar

Pineapple in Syrup

Fills a 4 cup (1 liter) jar

1 pineapple

1 lb 7 oz (650 g) superfine sugar

4 cups (1 liter) water

Peel, halve and core the pineapple. Slice each half of the pineapple into 3 even wedges, then reconstruct the fruit and place in a large sterilized jar (*see* page 248). Place the sugar and water in large pan over a high heat and bring just to a boil. Pour the liquid over the pineapple up to the brim of the jar and seal.

For the water-bath canning, line a large saucepan with cardboard, a kitchen towel or kitchen paper and fill with water. Bring to a gentle simmer. Place the sealed jar inside, topping up with boiling water if necessary to ensure the lid is covered by ½ inch (1 cm). Simmer for 30 minutes then remove from the heat, leaving the jar in the saucepan to cool completely before removing and storing.

Store for up to 1 year in a cool place. Once opened, store in the fridge and use within 1 month.

Plums in Syrup

Fills a 4 cup (1 liter) jar

1 lb 2 oz (500 g) plums, pitted and quartered

seeds of 1 vanilla pod

4 cups (1 liter) water

9 oz (250 g) superfine sugar

Place the plums and vanilla seeds in a large sterilized jar (*see* page 248) and set aside. Place the sugar and water in a large pan over a high heat and bring just to a boil. Pour the liquid over the plums up to the brim of the jar and seal. Process following the water-bath canning instructions (*see* left). Store for up to 1 year in a cool place. Once opened, store in the fridge and use within 1 month.

251

Apple Compote

Fills a 22 oz (250 ml) jar

1 lb 12 oz (800 g) cox apples, peeled,
    cored and roughly chopped

2 tablespoons lemon juice

1 oz (25 g) golden superfine sugar

1 pinch of ground cinnamon

Place the apples, lemon juice and superfine sugar in
a large pan over a medium heat. Bring to a simmer,
then cover the pan and cook over a low heat for 25
minutes, until soft and golden. Transfer the mixture
to a blender with a pinch of cinnamon and blend
until completely smooth. Transfer to a sterilized
jar (*see* page 248) and seal. Process for 25 minutes
following the water-bath canning instructions (*see*
page 251). This can be eaten warm or cooled. Once
opened, store in the fridge and use within 1 month.

White Peach Jam with Cordial

Fills a 27 oz (800 ml) jar

2 lb 4 oz (1 kg) white peaches, stoned
    and roughly chopped

14 oz (400 g) superfine sugar

3 tablespoons elderflower cordial

Place the peaches, superfine sugar and cordial in
a large pan over a medium heat. Bring to a boil,
then reduce the heat to a simmer and cook for
20 minutes, stirring frequently. If you prefer a
smooth jam, place in a blender and blend until
smooth before transferring to a sterilized jar (*see*
page 248) and sealing. Process for 25 minutes
following the water-bath canning instructions (*see*
page 251). Store unopened for up to 1 year in a
cool place. Once opened, store in the fridge and
use within 1 month.

Quince Pâte de Fruit

Emily: My grandmother has always made delicious quince pâte. This is her precious recipe.

Fills a 2 lb (900 g) cake pan

2 lb 4 oz (1 kg) quince, peeled, cored and quartered

1 lb 10 oz (750 g) superfine sugar, plus extra for coating

seeds of 1 vanilla pod

Line a large round or rectangular cake pan or lipped baking dish with parchment paper and set aside until needed. Place the quince in a large pan over a medium heat with enough water to just cover the fruit. Bring to a boil, then reduce the heat to a simmer and cook for 25 minutes, until tender. Drain the fruit and transfer to a blender, then blend until completely smooth. Return the purée to the pan along with the sugar and vanilla seeds and cook over a medium heat, stirring continuously, until the sugar has dissolved and the mixture has started to bubble. Turn the heat down to a gentle simmer and leave to cook, stirring occasionally, for around 30–40 minutes, until the mixture has thickened and darkened to a deep orange color. Pour the mixture into your prepared cake pan or baking sheet and leave to cool and set. This can then be cut into pieces and rolled in sugar to be enjoyed as a sweet snack or left as it is for use with savory dishes. Store in the fridge and use within 1 year.

Savory Preserves

Preserved Peas

Fills a 1¾ pint (1 liter) jar

4 lb 8 oz (2 kg) fresh peas, shelled

4 cups (1 liter) water, plus extra
for boiling peas

¾ oz (20 g) salt

Bring a large pan of water to a boil, add the peas and blanch for 4 minutes, until tender. Rinse immediately in iced water, then drain. Transfer the cooked and cooled peas to a large sterilized jar (*see* page 248) and set aside. Place the water and salt in a large pan over a high heat, bring to a boil, then immediately pour the liquid over the peas and seal. Process following the water-bath canning instructions (*see* page 251). Store unopened for up to 1 year in a cool place. Once opened, store in the fridge and use within 1 month.

Preserved Runner Beans

Fills a 1¾ pint (1 liter) jar

2 lb 4 oz (1 kg) fresh runner beans, trimmed

4 cups (1 liter) water, plus extra for boiling beans

¾ oz (20 g) salt

Bring a large pan of water to a boil, add the beans and blanch until tender. Rinse immediately in iced water, then drain. Transfer the cooked and cooled beans to a large sterilized jar (*see* page 248) and set aside. Place the water and salt in a large pan over a high heat, bring to a boil, then immediately pour the liquid over the peas and seal. Process following the water-bath canning instructions (*see* page 251). Store unopened for up to 1 year in a cool place. Once opened, store in the fridge and use within 1 month.

Artichokes in Vinegar

Fills a 18 oz (500ml) jar

1 cup (250 ml) water

1 cup (250 ml) white wine vinegar

juice of ½ lemon

10–15 small artichoke hearts

10 black peppercorns

1 small bay leaf

1 cup (250 ml) olive oil

salt

Place the water, white wine vinegar, lemon juice and a pinch of salt in a large pan over a medium heat. Bring just to a boil then add the artichoke hearts and cook until tender, approximately 12 minutes. Strain the artichokes, discarding the cooking liquid, and set aside to dry on a clean kitchen towel. Once dry, place the artichokes in a sterilized jar (*see* page 248) with the peppercorns and bay leaf, then top up the jar with the olive oil and seal. Process following the water-bath canning instructions (*see* page 251). Store unopened for up to 1 year in a cool place. Once opened, store in the fridge and use within 1 month.

Tomato and Basil Sauce

Giselle: I think it's safe to say on behalf of all my siblings that the tomato season was by far the worst when we were children. The whole family seemed always to be covered head-to-toe with tomato juice and seeds at this time as preserving our crop was a shared task and took several messy days.

Fills a 1¾ pint (1 liter) jar

2 tablespoons olive oil

1 onion, finely chopped

2 garlic cloves, finely chopped

4 lb 8 oz (2 kg) ripe tomatoes

1 thyme sprig

½ bunch of basil, leaves ripped

½ teaspoon dried chili flakes

1 pinch of superfine sugar

salt and freshly ground black pepper

Place the olive oil in a wide shallow pan over a medium heat. Once hot, add the onion and garlic and cook, stirring continuously, for 3 minutes, until soft and translucent. Add the rest of the ingredients to the pan and season to taste. Bring to a gentle simmer and leave to cook for 30 minutes, until reduced by half. Transfer to a sterilized jar (*see* page 248) and seal. Process following the water-bath canning instructions (*see* page 251). This can be used as it is for a pasta sauce or blended until smooth to make a great tomato base for pizzas. Once opened, store in the fridge and use within 1 month.

Chicken Liver Pâté

Giselle: Chicken liver pâté is a great favorite of Emily's and is something my mother would make and store. She hated waste and would always be sure to use up any chicken livers. This is delicious spread thickly over toasted baguette.

Fills two 12 oz (350 ml) jars

7 oz (200 g) butter, softened

1 lb 2 oz (500 g) trimmed chicken livers

3 shallots, finely chopped

1 thyme sprig

3½ oz (100 ml) port

¼ cup (50 ml) cognac

salt and freshly ground black pepper

Heat 1 tablespoon of the butter in a frying pan over a medium heat. Once melted and bubbling, add the chicken livers, shallots and thyme sprig and sauté for 3–4 minutes, depending on size. Deglaze the pan with the port and reduce by half. Transfer to a bowl and set aside to cool to room temperature. Once cooled, transfer the mixture to a blender and blend until smooth, gradually incorporating the remaining butter and the cognac. Once smooth and fully incorporated, season the pâté to taste and transfer the mixture to 2 sterilized jars (*see* page 248) and seal. Place in the fridge overnight to set. Store in the fridge and use within 3 days.

257

Classic Desserts

Emily

A family dinner doesn't feel complete unless it ends with something sweet. Even following the heaviest of meals, after a little break, there's always room for a little something. When we're on holiday in France, we always take plenty of time to talk and laugh over dinner and have a dessert every day.

Cakes and desserts bring our whole family together and all three of us love simple old-fashioned dishes the best. For all the new ingredients and techniques we've embraced in our cooking, we always come back to traditional recipes when it comes to the sweet course. Our *beignets* (see page 274), *clafoutis* (see page 286) and fruit tarts (see page 287) taste exactly like those my grandmother used to cook and are perfect just the way they are.

There are some exceptions, though. I've discovered that eggplants are a wonderful, if unlikely, addition to chocolate pots (see page 293), adding texture and interest; Oreos give a wonderfully contemporary twist to classic Spanish doughnuts (see page 268); and my feather-light *Gâteau de Savoie* (see page 264) is lighter than the version that my mother used to eat as a child.

Gâteau de Savoie

This is an extremely light and airy cake that is delicious with tea and coffee, toasted at breakfast time or served with clotted cream.

Serves 8

2¼ oz (60 g) unsalted butter, melted, plus extra for greasing

8 oz (225 g) superfine sugar

7½ oz (210 g) egg whites

5 oz (140 g) egg yolks

2¾ oz (80 g) cornstarch

2¾ oz (80 g) plain flour

1½ teaspoons baking powder

Preheat the oven to 325°F (160°C), and grease the inside of a deep 8 inch (20 cm) round cake pan with melted butter. Sprinkle ½ oz (15 g) of the sugar over the surface of the pan and set aside.

Place the egg whites in a large mixing bowl or the bowl of a stand mixer and whisk to firm peaks. With the whisk still running, gradually add 4½ oz (120 g) of the sugar to form a smooth, glossy meringue. Set aside.

In another bowl, whisk the egg yolks with the remaining sugar, until pale and thickened. Pour this mixture into the egg white mixture and carefully fold the two mixtures together until just combined. It is very important to be gentle here — if you are too vigorous you will knock the air out

of your mixture and end up with a flat, dense cake. Sift the cornstarch, flour and baking powder over the egg mixture, then carefully fold them through until combined. Pour the mixture into your prepared cake pan and transfer to the oven to cook for 35 minutes, until well risen, golden and springy to the touch.

Set the cake aside for 10 minutes before removing it from the pan. The cake is delicious served warm or cold.

Classic Honey Madeleines

Dainty, bite-sized madeleines make a delicious tea-time treat or gift. In France, the family madeleine recipe is a closely guarded secret, but we are sharing ours with you here.

Makes 60 madeleines

3 oz (85 g) egg yolks

10½ oz (300 g) beaten egg

seeds of 1 vanilla pod

9 oz (250 g) superfine sugar

9 oz (250 g) plain flour, plus extra for flouring

2½ teaspoons baking powder

½ oz (15 g) good-quality honey

10½ oz (300 g) unsalted clarified butter

1½ teaspoons salt

butter, for greasing

The day before you want to bake the madeleines, whisk the egg yolks, beaten eggs and vanilla seeds together in a large mixing bowl. Add the sugar and continue to beat until pale and foamy. Sift the flour, baking powder and salt into the bowl and carefully fold in until just incorporated. Melt the honey and clarified butter together in the microwave, then pour into the madeleine batter and stir until just combined. Cover with plastic wrap and transfer to the fridge overnight.

The next day, preheat your oven to 450°F (230°C), and butter and flour your madeleine molds (if you are using silicone molds, they will not need to be greased). The easiest way to fill the molds with the batter is by using a disposable piping bag without a nozzle, but a tablespoon will also work well. Fill each mold to around the halfway level, being as even as you can.

To cook the madeleines perfectly, you need to use a timer. Transfer the madeleines to the oven to cook for 3 minutes, then turn off the oven for a further 2 minutes. Finally, turn the oven on again at 350°F (180°C), and leave to cook for another 10 minutes, turning the tray halfway through the cooking time, until well risen and golden. Turning the oven off and then on again creates the bumps in the middles of the madeleines.

Leave the madeleines to cool for 10 minutes in their pan before turning out. Do not let them cool entirely in their tins as they will stick and be impossible to remove cleanly. These are best eaten on the day they are made.

Oreo Churros with Coconut and Vanilla Chantilly

This modern take on the classic Spanish doughnuts will be a hit with young and old alike. The coconut Chantilly also makes an excellent icing and has the added bonus of being dairy free.

Serves 4–6

For the coconut Chantilly:

1 can full-fat coconut milk 14 oz (400 ml)

seeds of 1 vanilla pod

1 teaspoon honey

For the Oreo churros:

15 Oreo cookies

1 tablespoon superfine sugar

8½ oz (240 ml) water

1 teaspoon salt

1 oz (30 g) unsalted butter

2¼ oz (60 g) plain flour, sifted

1 egg

neutral oil, such as rapeseed or sunflower, for shallow frying

For the sugar coating:

1 tablespoon ground cinnamon

2 tablespoons superfine sugar

Start preparing the coconut Chantilly the day before you want to serve the churros. Pour the coconut milk into a bowl and place in the fridge overnight. The next day the milk should have separated into a thick cream and a thin milk. Drain off the milk (this can be used to make smoothies) and place the remaining cream in a large mixing bowl. Using an electric whisk, whisk the coconut cream for 3 minutes, until light and fluffy. Stir in the vanilla seeds and honey and set aside in the fridge until ready to use.

To make the churros, separate the 2 halves of each Oreo and scrape out and discard the filling. Place the dark shells in a food processor and process to a fine black powder. Set aside.

Place the sugar, water, salt and butter in a large pan over a medium heat. When the butter has melted and the liquid has just started to boil, remove the pan from the heat and tip in the flour and black Oreo powder. Mix thoroughly with a wooden spoon until the mixture forms a ball and pulls away cleanly from the sides of the pan. Add the egg to the mixture and continue to beat until you obtain a smooth paste.

Line a baking sheet that will fit in your freezer with parchment paper and fill a piping bag fitted with a large star-shaped nozzle with the churros mixture. Pipe straight 4 inch (10 cm) churros onto the baking sheet until all of the mixture is used up. Transfer the baking sheet to the freezer for around 30 minutes, until the churros are firm enough to lift off the parchment paper by hand.

Meanwhile, combine the ingredients for the sugar coating in a small bowl and set aside until needed.

Around 10 minutes before you want to start frying, half fill a frying pan with oil. Heat the oil to a temperature of 365°F (185°C) then, working in small batches, carefully lower the churros into the oil and cook for 6 minutes, turning halfway through cooking. The churros should be crispy and golden on the outside with a light fluffy center. Transfer the cooked churros to paper towels to drain off any excess oil, then roll in the sugar coating whilst still hot.

Serve the churros warm with the coconut Chantilly alongside for dipping.

268

Beignets aux Pommes

These deliciously warming apple fritters are perfect for winter days when you want to bundle up and hunker down inside to escape the cold.

Serves 4

1 cup (250 ml) whole milk

1 vanilla pod, halved and seeds removed

5½ oz (150 g) plain flour

1½ teaspoons baking powder

2 egg yolks

2 tablespoons vegetable or sunflower oil

½ oz (15 g) superfine sugar

3–4 apples ("Golden Delicious" or "Pink Lady" work well), peeled, cored and cut into ¼ inch (5 mm) slices

sunflower or corn oil, for deep-frying

icing sugar, for dusting

Place the milk in a medium pan over a low heat. Add the vanilla pod and seeds to the pan and leave on the heat until just starting to simmer. Do not allow the milk to boil. Remove the pan from the heat and set aside until lukewarm for the flavors to infuse.

Meanwhile, sift the flour and baking powder into a large mixing bowl, then add the egg yolks, oil and superfine sugar. Discard the vanilla pod from the milk, then gradually whisk the milk into the flour and egg mixture until fully incorporated. If you have any lumps, continue to whisk until you have a smooth liquid batter. Cover the mixture with plastic wrap and set aside to rest for 1 hour in the fridge.

Around 15 minutes before you want to start frying, heat your oil to 350°F (180°C). If using a deep-fat fryer use the amount recommended by the manufacturer (most domestic varieties vary between 4–12 cups (1–3 liters); if using a deep pan, 6 cups (1.5 liters) should be sufficient. The oil needs to be around 4 inches (10 cm) deep, but nowhere near the top lip of the pan.

When the oil is up to temperature, dip batches of the apple slices in the batter and then carefully transfer them to the hot oil. Be careful not to overload your fryer or pan as the fritters will not cook evenly. Cook for 5 minutes, turning the slices over halfway through the cooking time. Transfer the cooked fritters to a plate lined with paper towels to drain off any excess oil while you cook the remainder of the apple slices.

Once all of the fritters are cooked, dust generously with icing sugar and serve warm.

Brioche and Butter Pudding

This is a simple recipe that the whole family will enjoy. It is a great way to use up any leftover bread you have in the house and you can substitute the brioche with whatever you have to hand — croissants or panettone work well, but result in a slightly richer pudding. Nutmeg, cinnamon or chopped nuts also make a welcome addition.

Serves 4

1 oz (30 g) raisins

1 tablespoon dark rum

6¼ oz (180 ml) whole milk

3 eggs

3½ oz (100 g) superfine sugar, plus
    extra for sprinkling

seeds of 1 vanilla pod

8½ oz (240 g) sliced brioche

½ oz (15 g) unsalted butter, diced,
    plus extra for greasing

Preheat the oven to 375°F (190°C), and grease a round 8 inch (20 cm) baking dish with butter.

Place the raisins in a small bowl and pour over the rum. Set aside to macerate while you prepare the rest of the dish.

Place the milk in a small pan over a low heat. Bring just to a boil, then immediately remove from the heat. Set aside for a couple of minutes to cool slightly.

Meanwhile, place the eggs, sugar and vanilla seeds in a large mixing bowl and whisk until pale and frothy. Once the milk has cooled slightly (if it is too hot it will scramble the eggs), gradually pour it into the egg mixture, constantly whisking, until fully combined. Working one slice at a time,

dip the brioche into the custard and leave to soak for around a minute. Neatly arrange the soaked brioche in your prepared baking dish, ensuring it is well filled with no gaps.

Pour the rum and raisin mixture into the custard and then pour this whole mixture over the top of your arranged brioche. Scatter a little sugar over the pudding and dot the cubes of butter over the top. Transfer to the oven to bake for 40–45 minutes, until golden brown and crisp. Serve hot.

Mini-Canelés Bordelais

This is a speciality of the region of Bordeaux, very often served with coffee, but equally delicious served as a dessert with ice cream or crème anglaise alongside. The batter needs to be made a day ahead, but if you're organized they are more than worth the effort.

Makes 60 *mini-canelés*

2 cups (500 ml) whole milk

1¾ oz (50 g) unsalted butter, plus extra for greasing

1 vanilla pod, halved and seeds removed

7 oz (200 g) superfine sugar

2 eggs and 2 egg yolks

3½ oz (100 g) plain flour

1 tablespoon dark rum

pinch of salt

crème anglaise (**see** page 293) or ice cream, to serve (optional)

The day before you want to serve the canelés, place the milk in a large pan over a low heat. Add the butter and vanilla pod and seeds and leave on the heat until the butter has just melted. Do not allow the milk to boil. Once the butter has melted into the milk, remove the pan from the heat and set aside for a few minutes for the flavors to infuse.

Meanwhile, place the sugar, eggs and egg yolks in a large mixing bowl and whisk until pale. Sift the flour into the mixture, then add the rum and a pinch of salt and mix to combine.

Remove the vanilla pods from the milk mixture and discard. Whisking all the time, gradually pour the lukewarm milk into the flour and egg mixture until fully incorporated. If there are any lumps, continue to whisk until you have a smooth liquid batter. Cover the mixture with plastic wrap and transfer to the fridge overnight.

The next day, preheat your oven to 500°F (260°C), and grease your *mini canelés* molds with

butter (if you are using silicone molds, they won't need to be greased). Remove the batter mixture from the fridge and stir briefly to ensure it is well combined. Pour the batter mixture into the molds, stopping just short of the top to allow a little room for the *canelés* to rise during cooking.

Transfer the *canelés* to the oven and cook for 8 minutes, then immediately reduce the temperature to 350°F (180°C), and leave to cook for a further 40 minutes, until the tops are dark brown and crisp to the touch. Set aside to cool for at least 10 minutes.

Once they have cooled slightly, remove the canelés from their molds and serve warm with crème anglaise or ice cream alongside.

Hazelnut and Blueberry Cookies

A good cookie recipe is a must for any cook: they can be thrown together quickly, travel well and everyone loves them. You could even portion the dough and freeze it for baking at a moment's notice.

Makes 25 cookies

6 oz (175 g) butter, softened

3½ oz (100 g) demerara (raw) sugar

1¾ oz (50 g) superfine sugar

2 eggs, beaten

2 teaspoons vanilla extract

9 oz (250 g) large rolled oats

5¾ oz (160 g) dried blueberries

4½ oz (125 g) chopped hazelnuts, lightly toasted

4½ oz (125 g) plain flour

1 teaspoon baking soda

½ teaspoon salt

Preheat the oven to 350°F (180°C), and line 2 or 3 large baking sheets with parchment paper.

In a large bowl, cream the butter and both sugars together until light and creamy. Add the eggs and vanilla extract and beat until well combined. Add the oats, blueberries and hazelnuts and stir to combine. Finally, sift over the flour and baking soda and add the salt. Mix until everything is well combined and the ingredients are evenly distributed.

Using your hands or an ice-cream scoop, divide the mixture into 20 even-sized balls. Lay the balls on your prepared baking trays and press them down slightly with your fingertips to form cookie shapes. These will spread during cooking, so don't place them too close to each other. If you don't have enough baking trays or your oven is small, you will need to bake in batches.

Transfer the cookies to the oven to bake for 10–15 minutes, depending on how soft you like your cookies. Transfer to a wire rack to cool and serve warm or at room temperature.

Rice Pudding

This classic dessert is a guaranteed crowd pleaser and very simple to prepare. If you are lucky enough to own a wood-fired oven, the smoky taste imparted by the embers will add an extra layer of flavor that will be sure to surprise and delight your guests.

Serves 4

20 oz (600 ml) whole milk

2½ oz (70 g) pudding rice

1 oz (30 g) superfine sugar

1 pinch of ground cardamom

1 vanilla pod, halved and seeds removed

¼ oz (10 g) salted butter, cubed

2 tablespoons whipped cream (optional)

Preheat the oven to 275°F (140°C).

Place the milk, rice, sugar, cardamom and vanilla pod and seeds in a medium saucepan over a low heat. Bring just to a boil, then immediately remove the pan from the heat. Remove and discard the vanilla pod, then pour the mixture into a deep ovenproof baking dish. Transfer the pudding to the oven and leave to cook, uncovered, for 45 minutes.

After 45 minutes, remove the pudding from the oven and give the mixture a stir. Dot the cubes of butter over the surface of the pudding, then return it to the oven and cook for a further 35 minutes, until all of the liquid has been absorbed and the rice on top has turned a light golden brown.

This is best enjoyed lukewarm or cooled, so set the pudding aside for at least 30 minutes before serving. For added indulgence, fold the whipped cream through the pudding before serving.

Classic Chocolate Mousse

Chocolate mousse is easy to make but always feels decadent and sophisticated, which makes it the perfect make-ahead dinner-party dessert.

Serves 6

9 oz (250 g) good-quality dark
    chocolate (at least 70 percent
    cocoa solids)

2½ oz (70 g) unsalted butter

6 eggs, separated

cocoa powder, to decorate

Place the chocolate and butter in a heatproof glass bowl over a pan of barely simmering water, ensuring that the water does not touch the base of the bowl. Leave on the heat, stirring continuously, until the chocolate and butter are melted and glossy. Remove from the heat and set aside for 5 minutes to cool.

Meanwhile, place the egg whites in a large bowl and whisk to stiff peaks with an electric whisk.

Once the chocolate mixture is cooled, add the egg yolks to the bowl and whisk to combine. Now add one-quarter of the beaten egg whites to the bowl and fold in to loosen the mixture. Add the remainder of the egg whites and carefully fold in until fully incorporated. It is important not to be too vigorous here or you will knock the air out of your mousse. Place in the fridge for at least 4 hours to set.

When ready to serve, spoon a large quenelle of the mousse onto each serving plate and decorate with sifted cocoa powder.

Apple Cake

The apples in this cake make it deliciously moist, ensuring that it keeps well and can be enjoyed over several days with a relaxing afternoon cup of coffee.

Serves 6

2¾ oz (80 g) unsalted butter, softened, plus extra for greasing

10½ oz (300 g) self-raising flour, plus extra for dusting

1 egg, beaten

5½ oz (150 g) superfine sugar

3 "Cox" or "Bramley" apples, peeled, cored and chopped into bite-sized pieces

whipped cream, to serve (optional)

Preheat the oven 350°F (180°C). Grease the inside of a deep 8 inch (20 cm) round cake pan with butter and dust the inside of the pan with a coating of flour.

Whisk the egg and sugar in a large mixing bowl until pale, then add the butter and continue to whisk until fully incorporated. Sift the flour into the bowl, then add the chopped apples. Mix until all of the ingredients are fully incorporated and then pour the batter into the prepared cake pan. Transfer to the oven for 30 minutes, until the cake is well risen, golden and springy to the touch and an inserted skewer comes out clean. Leave to cool for at least 10 minutes before removing the cake from its pan.

This cake will keep for several days, but is best enjoyed lukewarm from the oven with whipped cream on the side.

Cherry *Clafoutis*

This dessert is always impressive, yet is deceptively simple to make. Beautifully sweet cherries are only available for a couple of months every year, but that just makes this classic dish even more special.

Serves 6

1 tablespoon butter, for greasing

5½ oz (150 g) fresh cherries, pitted

3 eggs

seeds from 1 vanilla pod

5 oz (140 g) superfine sugar

1 tablespoon soft brown sugar

2¼ oz (60 g) plain flour

7½ oz (215 ml) whole milk

pinch of salt

icing sugar, for dusting

Preheat the oven 350°F (180°C), and grease the inside of an ovenproof baking dish just large enough to hold all of the cherries in a single layer with butter. Lay the cherries in the base of the dish and set aside.

Place the eggs, vanilla seeds and both sugars in a large bowl and whisk together until well combined. Sift in the flour and salt and mix to combine. Pour in the milk and whisk to a smooth batter.

Pour the batter into the prepared baking dish over the top of the cherries, then transfer to the oven to bake for 35–40 minutes, until lightly risen, golden and an inserted skewer comes out clean.

Dust the clafoutis generously with icing sugar and serve warm.

Tarte Reine Claude

This delicious dessert is the perfect middle ground between a summery fruit tart and a warming winter dessert. Greengages are a type of plum that are common in France, but can be harder to find elsewhere. Other stone fruit would work just as well.

Serves 6–8

For the pastry:

3½ oz (100 g) unsalted butter, at room temperature

3½ oz (100 g) superfine sugar

1 egg and 2 egg yolks

7 oz (200 g) plain flour

For the filling:

1 egg and 1 egg yolk

2¾ oz (80 g) superfine sugar

1 oz (25 g) plain flour

2¾ oz (75 g) finely ground almonds

pinch of salt

8 oz (225 g) crème fraîche

1 lb 2 oz (500 g) greengages, pitted

To make the pastry, place the butter and sugar in a bowl and mix until pale, light and fluffy. Add the eggs and egg yolks and mix to incorporate. Sift in the flour and mix to form a soft pastry. Wrap the pastry in plastic wrap and transfer to the fridge for 2 hours before using.

While the pastry is chilling, preheat the oven to 350°F (180°C).

To make the tart filling, place the egg, egg yolk and sugar in a large mixing bowl and whisk until pale and airy. Sift the flour, ground almonds and salt into the bowl and whisk to combine. Add the crème fraîche and whisk the mixture until smooth and well combined. Set aside.

Once the pastry has finished chilling, roll it out on a lightly floured surface to a thickness of ¼ inch (5 mm). Line a 9 inch (23 cm) loose-based tart pan with the pastry, then line the pastry with parchment paper and fill with baking beans.

Transfer to the oven to blind bake for 15 minutes, until lightly golden, removing the parchment paper and baking beans for the last 5 minutes of cooking.

Lay the prepared greengages in the base of the pastry shell, then pour over the filling mixture. It's nice if a few of the greengages are peeking through the filling after cooking, so you may want to keep a few back to place on top. Transfer to the oven for 25–30 minutes, until golden brown and lightly risen.

Leave the tart to rest for 10 minutes before removing from its pan. This is delicious served warm from the oven or left to cool and served at room temperature.

Carrot Cake

This delicious cake is packed with chewy dried cranberries and crunchy pecans, while the carrots make it incredibly moist and bring a natural sweetness. This recipe makes two loaves, because one is never enough!

makes 2 loaves

butter, for greasing

For the dry ingredients:

4½ oz (125 g) plain flour

4½ oz (125 g) whole-wheat flour

1 tablespoon baking powder

5½ oz (150 g) golden superfine sugar

1 tablespoon baking soda

1 teaspoon salt

2 teaspoons ground cinnamon

1 teaspoon ground ginger

1 teaspoon ground nutmeg

seeds of 1 vanilla pod

For the wet ingredients:

4 eggs, beaten

14 oz (400 g) carrots, grated

5½ oz (150 g) chopped pecans

1¾ oz (50 g) dried cranberries

10 oz (300 ml) melted coconut oil

Preheat the oven to 350°F (180°C), and grease two 2 lb (900 g) loaf pans with butter.

Sift the flours and baking powder into a large mixing bowl, then add the rest of the dry ingredients. Stir to combine, then make a well in the center and add all of the wet ingredients. Mix everything together until well combined and divide the mixture between your prepared loaf pans. Transfer to the oven to cook for 45 minutes, until golden, well risen and an inserted skewer comes out clean.

Leave the cakes to cool in their pans for 10 minutes before turning out onto wire racks and leaving to cool completely. Serve at room temperature.

Chocolate and Eggplant Pots

This updated version of a classic chocolate mousse requires a bit of a leap of faith, but the results speak for themselves. Eggplant may seem like a very odd addition to a dessert, but its bitterness perfectly complements the silky dark chocolate.

Serves 6

1 large eggplant, peeled and cut into 1 inch (2.5 cm) dice

5¾ oz (160 g) good-quality dark chocolate (at least 70 percent cocoa solids)

For the crème anglaise:

5 oz (150 ml) whole milk

5 oz (150 ml) whipping cream

3 egg yolks

1 oz (30 g) superfine sugar

Preheat the oven to 350°F (180°C), and line a baking sheet with parchment paper.

Spread the eggplant over the prepared baking sheet and transfer to the oven for 25 minutes, until soft and pulpy. Transfer to a blender and blend until smooth. If the mixture is not perfectly smooth, press it through a sieve to achieve a smooth purée. Set aside.

To make the crème anglaise, place the milk and cream in a medium pan over a low heat. Bring just to a boil, then immediately remove from the heat. Set aside for a couple of minutes to cool slightly.

Meanwhile, place the egg yolks and sugar in a large mixing bowl and whisk until pale and frothy. Once the milk has cooled slightly (if it is too hot it will scramble the eggs), gradually pour it into the egg mixture, constantly whisking, until fully combined. Pour the mixture back into the pan and place over a low heat. Using a kitchen thermometer, continue to whisk the mixture until its temperature has reached 180°F (82°C), at this point the mixture should have thickened slightly.

Break the chocolate into another large mixing bowl and pour over one-third of the crème anglaise, stir until the chocolate has almost melted, then add another third and stir to combine. Finally, pour in the last of the crème anglaise and stir until fully combined.

Add 9 oz (250 g) of the eggplant purée to the mixture and stir until fully incorporated. Divide the mixture between 6 ramekins and transfer to the fridge to set for at least 2 hours before serving.

293

Index

Acknowledgments

Thank you to Charlotte and Andrew who got the ball rolling and guided us through our first steps. We are also grateful for Jinny's help, who assisted us in putting the appropriate words to our never-ending family stories.

This book wouldn't have been the same without our fantastic group of girls. Helen, Rosie, Ellie, Linda and Jen made this experience extra special. Our lunch feasts during the shoots will never be forgotten.

Finally, we are thankful to all our friends and family that helped us by sampling every single recipe in this book.

Hopefully these recipes won't be pinched by … you know who.